This is the Word of the Lord

Year B

This is the Word of the Lord

Year B
The Year of Mark

EDITED BY ROBIN DUCKWORTH, SM

London
BIBLE READING FELLOWSHIP

Oxford New York Toronto Melbourne
OXFORD UNIVERSITY PRESS · 1981

Oxford University Press, Walton Street, Oxford OX2 6DP
London Glasgow New York Toronto
Delhi Bombay Calcutta Madras Karachi
Kuala Lumpur Singapore Hong Kong Tokyo
Nairobi Dar es Salaam Cape Town
Melbourne Wellington
and associate companies in
Beirut Berlin Ibadan Mexico City

Bible Reading Fellowship, St Michael's House,
2 Elizabeth Street, London SW1W 9RQ

British Library Cataloguing in Publication Data
        This is the word of the Lord.
        Year B: The year of Mark
        1. Lord's Supper   2. Lectionaries
        I. Duckworth, Robin
        II. Bible Reading Fellowship
        264'.34   BV825.5
        ISBN 0-19-826662-6

Typeset by Phoenix Photosetting, Chatham
Printed in Hong Kong

Contents

Chronological tables

Maps

Names for Sundays in Ordinary Time

Some churchpeople will be familiar with other names for these
Sundays not within the two great seasons. Whatever the titles used –

Sundays after Epiphany, then Sundays after Pentecost, for example – the readings in the three-year scheme are substantially the same. In all the churches there is careful adjustment so that after the interruption by Lent–Easter the readings begin again together.

The table on page 41 supplies information which makes clear the set of readings to be used, no matter what title is common for Sundays out of season.

Readings in the Episcopal Church (USA)

The new Prayer Book's Lectionary fits with Sundays in Ordinary Time as follows:

Ordinary Time	Sundays after Epiphany	Propers
2nd	2nd	
3rd	3rd	
4th	4th	
5th	5th	
6th	6th	1 (closest to May 11)
7th	7th	2 (closest to May 18)
8th	8th	3 (closest to May 25)
9th		4 (closest to June 1)
10th		5 (closest to June 8)
11th		6 (closest to June 15)
12th		7 (closest to June 22)
13th		8 (closest to June 29)
14th		9 (closest to July 6)
15th		10 (closest to July 13)
16th		11 (closest to July 20)
17th		12 (closest to July 27)
18th		13 (closest to Aug. 3)
19th		14 (closest to Aug. 10)
20th		15 (closest to Aug. 17)
21st		16 (closest to Aug. 24)

22nd	17 (closest to Aug. 31)
23rd	18 (closest to Sept. 7)
24th	19 (closest to Sept. 14)
25th	20 (closest to Sept. 21)
26th	21 (closest to Sept. 28)
27th	22 (closest to Oct. 5)
28th	23 (closest to Oct. 12)
29th	24 (closest to Oct. 19)
30th	25 (closest to Oct. 26)
31st	26 (closest to Nov. 2)
32nd	27 (closest to Nov. 9)
33rd	28 (closest to Nov. 16)
Christ the King (Last Sunday of the Year)	29 (closest to Nov. 23)

Contributors

John Davies, Lecturer in Theology, University of Southampton. 24th–34th Sundays in Ordinary Time

Robin Duckworth, SM, Lecturer in Old Testament, Allen Hall, London. Year of Mark's Gospel; Gospel of John; The Psalms; Eastertide; Chronological Tables

W. Jardine Grisbrooke, Lecturer in Liturgy, St Mary's College, Oscott. Liturgical introductions

Raymond Hammer, Director, the Bible Reading Fellowship. The Epistles

Nilda Pettenuzzo, Tutor in Scripture, Heythrop College, University of London. Advent–Christmas

John Rogerson, Professor of Biblical Studies, University of Sheffield. 2nd–12th Sundays in Ordinary Time

Charles Southwood, Principal Lecturer in Religious Studies, Digby Stuart College of Education, London. Sundays in Lent; Holy Week

Norman Whybray, Professor of Hebrew and Old Testament Studies, University of Hull. 13th–23rd Sundays in Ordinary Time

Acknowledgement

The Responsorial Psalms are reproduced from the Grail version, © The Grail (England) 1963, published by Collins in Fontana Books, London, 1963. Used by permission.

Forewords

As President of the World Catholic Federation for the Biblical Apostolate, I welcome this small, handsome, and very useful book. No doubt it will find its way into the hands of priests and catechists as a valuable tool for the preparations of Sunday homilies.

But I sincerely hope also that it will reach many of the faithful. It is to them in particular that I wish to recommend this book highly. Reading the short commentaries on the Sunday readings and Gospels will greatly assist a deeper understanding of the texts, and in this way the Liturgy of the Word will become a more effective tool for evangelization.

✠ Paul Cardinal Zoungrana
President of W.C.F.B.A.

The adoption of the Three-Year Cycle of Readings in many churches around the world has opened the way to a more widely-based reading and exposition of the Scriptures at the Eucharist. We are finding it has great ecumenical significance too: it is splendid that Christians of different traditions are reflecting upon the same passages of the Bible on the same day.

The Bible Reading Fellowship is doing a valuable service to the clergy and laity alike in providing the helpful pithy commentaries on the weekly readings which are set out in this book.

I am very happy to commend this practical aid to our deeper appreciation of the eucharistic readings.

✠ Keith Rayner
Archbishop of Adelaide

Preface

This book is intended primarily for layfolk who wish to come to a better understanding of the content and message of the passages of Scripture used in the Sunday Lectionary. Therefore, the method employed has been to explain simply and clearly what the passages are about and to place them in their context. To do this the commentators have tried, as far as possible, to let the readings 'speak for themselves', so that the reader may obtain maximum benefit from them. Because personal interpretation has been avoided it is hoped that the explanation of the texts will be of special value to Bible-reading groups and study groups who are looking to understand the texts without being 'led' to a particular interpretation.

The supplementary sections have been added in order to give the user of this book a broader general base from which to work. We provide background information about the year's main Gospel, and also about John. This is because it both supplements the short Mark and features prominently in the Lent–Easter season. Similarly, for this last reason too, 1 John is included in the section introducing each of the epistles to be read. As the Responsorial Psalms are printed out within the commentary – both as a convenience and as an aid to devotion – the introduction has a brief survey of the background and content of the Psalms. It is hoped that the chronological tables will encourage that linking-up and setting-in-context which bring familiar words and events out into new historical light.

Finally, it should be remembered that Scripture is the word of God passed on to us in the words of men who lived at a particular time and in their own cultural environment. To know something of the background and context of the readings contained in the Lectionary paves the way for a better understanding of these 'words of men', which in turn, it is hoped, will lead to a greater awareness of the 'word of God'.

Robin Duckworth

INTRODUCTION

Year B: The Year of Mark's Gospel

To each year of its three-year cycle the Lectionary devotes one of the synoptic Gospels ('synoptic' means 'from the same viewpoint', and the first three Gospels are called synoptic because they look at their subject from the same point of view, broadly speaking), with supplementary material from the Gospel of St John (see below). Each Gospel does, however, have its own particular approach to the teaching of Christ, and it is by concentrating on a single Gospel throughout the liturgical year that the particular approach of each evangelist can be appreciated. Year B is devoted to the Gospel of Mark.

Mark, the shortest of the Gospels, was long regarded as no more than an abbreviation of Matthew, and so was comparatively neglected. Now, however, Mark is commonly recognized not only as the earliest canonical Gospel but also as one of the sources used by Matthew and Luke. Therefore it is a primary authority for our knowledge of the life and teaching of Jesus. The Gospel has been described as an expansion of the primitive *kerygma*, that is, the apostolic preaching (see, for example, Acts 10: 36–43), or as the recollection of an eyewitness set down in writing by his disciple and supplemented by material from other sources. Tradition has the apostle Peter as being the eyewitness, with his disciple as the Mark who figures in the New Testament (Acts 12: 25; Colossians 4: 10; 2 Timothy 4: 11, etc.). The Gospel is said to have been written in Rome after the death of Peter in AD 64, so a date of about 65 would not be far out. It was written for non-Jewish Christians. This is evident from the explanation of Aramaic expressions when they occur (e.g. 3: 17; 5: 41) and Jewish customs (e.g. 7: 3f.; 14: 12).

Characteristics

The outstanding feature of Mark's Gospel is the realism and vividness of the narrative. Though, as a whole, the work is shorter than Matthew and Luke, it is, nevertheless, often fuller and more

I

elaborate in its descriptions and abounds in graphic detail as to the manner, looks and gestures of Jesus. Along with this feature goes the candour of the narrative. Mark does not spare the disciples, nor does he gloss over their faults. This candour extends also to Jesus himself. The later evangelists tend to 'tone down' this candour of Mark. From the very opening verse Jesus is beyond question the Son of God, a note that resounds again and again throughout the Gospel. Indeed, as R. McL. Wilson points out: 'It is strong evidence for Mark's reliability that he shows so little tendency to recast his materials to match the theology of a later day' (Peake's Commentary, 1962, p. 800).

Plan of the Gospel

The core of Mark's Gospel is the apostolic proclamation (see above) that Jesus began his ministry in Galilee, worked miracles, was crucified, has been raised from the dead and is now Lord and Christ (see particularly Peter's sermon to the household of Cornelius, Acts 10: 36–43). The first half of the Gospel expands the historical part of the proclamation, giving an account of Jesus in Galilee, his healing, and the power and authority of his personality. All this leads up to the climax and turning-point of the Gospel: the incident at Caesarea Philippi where Peter, in answer to Jesus' question: 'Who do you say that I am?', replies, 'You are the Christ'. The second half then begins with Mark explaining a new feature: the Son of Man must suffer and die. Jesus' life now moves steadily on to his last hour. Three times he predicts his passion while he leads his disciples to Jerusalem, the Holy City, to consummate his work by death. Thus the second half of the Gospel is a preparation for the account of the Passion which takes the main place in and makes up a substantial part of the entire book. Yet another climax is reached in the Passion account when the centurion confesses: 'Truly this man was the Son of God' (15: 39). Finally the Gospel ends with accounts of the appearances of the risen Christ which confirm the confession and consummate the faith of the disciples.

A general outline of the Gospel is as follows:
1. Introduction: preaching of the Baptist; baptism of

Theology

Mark's Gospel is dominated by a paradox: how Jesus, while remaining misunderstood and rejected by men, was, at the same time, God's triumphant envoy. The heart of the Gospel is the manifestation of the crucified Messiah. On the one hand Jesus is acknowledged as the Son of God by the Father (1: 11), by the demons (1: 24, etc.), even by men (15: 39). On the other hand, he suffers apparent frustration, rejection by the public (5: 40; 6: 2f.), antagonism of the Jewish leaders (2: 1–3: 6, etc.), even lack of understanding by his disciples (4: 13, etc.). All this is the 'scandal' the Gospel is intent on explaining. This it does by contrasting it with the triumph of the resurrection, but also by showing that hostility was itself an integral part of God's mysterious plan. It was necessary that the Christ should suffer in order to redeem men (10: 45; 14: 24); Scripture had foretold this (9: 12; 14: 21, 49). Jesus laid down a way of humility and suffering. The Jews, however, expecting a victorious warrior-messiah, were not prepared for this answer to their hope. This was why Jesus wanted silence about his miracles and identity. Rather than call himself 'Messiah' (8: 29f.) Jesus took the modest and mysterious title 'Son of Man' (2: 10, etc.). This is what is known as the 'Messianic Secret' (1: 34, etc.) and is basic to Mark's presentation of the gospel. All this was not something Mark invented. After all, suffering was part of the history of Christ's life, but, in the light of faith and the resurrection, Mark sees it as full of meaning and he presents his insights to us, that we, too, may share his understanding.

The Gospel of John

The differences between John's Gospel and the other three have been noted right from the beginning. These differences apply to the narrative, to the discourses, and, indeed, to the whole plan and presentation of the Gospel. The two extreme views as to the reason for this are (1) that John wanted to supplement the other Gospels, and (2) that he never really knew the other Gospels at all. However, most scholars accept that John knew Mark and admit the possibility of his knowing Matthew and Luke. If, then, he did know the other Gospels' accounts, and had wished to supplement them, surely he would have harmonized his account with theirs? What John does is to presuppose that his readers know the synoptic tradition and he proceeds independently of it.

John's aim is to give theological depth to the portrait of Christ. 'While the synoptic Gospels tell of Jesus as he appeared to the eyes of his disciples during his ministry, John presents the picture of him that had taken shape before his own Spirit-enlightened gaze' (W. J. Harrington, *Explaining the Gospels*, 1978, p. 140).

John is known traditionally as 'the theologian'. But this term is not to be understood in the modern technical sense. Theology, according to the original meaning of the word, is nothing other than the knowledge of God and of divine things. It is in this sense that John is to be seen as the theologian 'because he has penetrated, more deeply than the other evangelists, the mystery of salvation; his Gospel is theological because it reveals to us, more intimately, the meaning of Christ' (Harrington, p. 141).

Plan and Structure

Scholars agree that the book is carefully planned. The plan, how-ever, must be quite subtle because there is no general agreement on it. What commentators do agree on is that the Gospel has a definite scheme and makes extensive use of symbolism. It is in its use of symbolism that we find the uniqueness of John's presentation. Each of the discourses arises from an episode and the episode is so con-structed as to symbolize the theme of the discourse. G. Allo and A.

Feuillet have summarized this symbolism as follows: John 1: 1 echoes Genesis 1: 1 and indicates that the incarnation of the Word initiates a new creation. There are seven days from the confession of the Baptist to the events at Cana. There are seven miracles. Water is a symbol of faith, of baptism, and of purification; wine is a symbol of blood, of sacrifice, of love, of the Eucharist. The episodes and discourse are arranged in eight pieces: (1) The miracle of Cana presents water and wine, baptism growing into union with the death of Jesus in the Eucharist. (2) In the cleansing of the Temple Jesus is revealed as the new temple. (3) The episodes of Nicodemus and the Samaritan present Jesus as the giver of the water of regeneration in baptism, offered to Jew and non-Jew, to man and woman. (4) Jesus gives life to the ruler's son. (5) The word of Christ to the paralytic has the power of healing water; he gives life to men and raises them from the dead. (6) Jesus is the bread of life, the new manna, in the Eucharist. (7) Jesus is the life and light of the world; he gives light to the blind man, in contrast to the spiritual darkness of the Jews, through the purification of water. (8) The climax of the presentation of Jesus as the resurrection and the life is the resurrection of Lazarus, who emerges from the darkness of the tomb to the light of life. (See J. L. McKenzie, *Dictionary of the Bible*, 1965/66, p. 450.)

Authorship and date

Early tradition attributes the authorship of the Gospel to John, son of Zebedee. And, indeed this is not incompatible with the evidence of the Gospel. However, authorship here may be taken loosely; the work may have come from John in substance and been re-worked and completed and published by his disciples. In other words, the original form of the Gospel need not be its present form. It is likely that material was added or touched up before the final editor completed the book in its present form. Probably, therefore, the final product is to be attributed not to John himself, but to his disciples. They inserted fragments that they did not wish to lose but did not know where to place. It is almost universally accepted today that 'the Gospel according to John' was written in the last decade of the first century.

Year B: The Epistles

Whilst the theme for each Sunday is drawn from the Old Testament reading and the Gospel, the reading of the Epistle enables us to identify with the early Church. The Epistles (letters) were written to be read out aloud in the churches and are usually directed towards the problems they were facing or the specific questions they had been asking. Note how doctrine and ethics are intermingled. Doctrine is no mere conceptual scheme; it becomes the basis of a specifically Christian life, in which love for God and love for one's neighbour are worked out in the *actual* situations of everyday living.

On Sundays in Ordinary Time the second readings consist of passages from five of the letters in the New Testament. It is suggested that individuals and groups read those chapters which are not set as lections, so that the readings can be put into context.

Sundays 2–6   1 Corinthians chs. 6–11
Sundays 7–14   2 Corinthians
Sundays 15–21   Ephesians
Sundays 22–26   James
Sundays 27–33   Hebrews chs. 2–10

We shall also be considering 1 John which is used in the Seasons.

1 Corinthians

The Church in Corinth had been established by Paul after his visit to Athens (see Acts 18: 1ff.) and became the chief centre of missionary activity in southern Greece. It was a busy seaport, a centre for trade and communication, and the letter reflects the moral problems linked with such a locality. Most of the converts came from the poorer classes of the city, but there were also well-to-do people among them (see 1 Corinthians 11: 22–34). The epistle as a whole is read through the three years of the Lectionary cycle. The chapters read in Year B are very diverse in character. There had been a case of litigation in the public courts in which both plaintiff and defendant had been Christians. Paul felt that such strife between Christians was shameful and hardly reflected upon the good name of the faith. It is preferable to suffer injustice than to do wrong, he asserts. He attacks sexual immorality, too, stressing that our bodies belong to God (see 1 Corinthians 6: 19–20).

From chapter 7 Paul deals with problems that had been raised with him in correspondence. Marriage, he insists, is a partnership to which both are committed. He does allow remarriage, in cases where the non-Christian partner will no longer maintain the marriage. In the light of the expectation of Christ's speedy return, Paul recommends celibacy, but sees no value in it if the 'celibate' is obsessed with sexual thoughts.

Next, he deals with the problem of meat sold in the public markets. Much of this had first been sacrificed at pagan altars. Were Christians to eat or not to eat? Paul can see no harm in eating, as pagan deities have no real existence, but, as he stresses time and time again, exercising one's own freedom is not the main criterion, but sensitivity towards one's fellow Christians.

Much of what is said about worship and the proprieties of dress belonged to Paul's time, but we are glad to have the earliest account of the Eucharist. He points to abuses which neglect the seriousness of the rite, in which we are to recognize Christ's body and blood.

2 Corinthians

This is one of the more personal of Paul's letters, in which doctrine is implicit rather than explicit. It provides us with information about Paul's movements, experiences and emotions during a period which is lightly passed over in Acts (see Acts 20: 1–3). Together with 1 Corinthians it gives us an insight into what a first-century church was like and also introduces us to first-century Christianity. It is probable that more than one letter is included and that 2 Corinthians 10–13 forms part of the somewhat severe letter to which Paul refers in 2 Corinthians 2: 3–4; 7: 12. These chapters certainly reflect a different situation from that suggested by the first nine chapters. It looks as if there had been an attack upon Paul's position after he had written 1 Corinthians and that his sharp letter was a response to criticisms of his mission and message (see 2 Corinthians 10: 7–12: 13). His retort led to a reconciliation between himself and the church, and this would account for the more peaceful tone of the early chapters of 2 Corinthians, in which he is chiefly concerned to repeat and re-emphasize the basis of his message and mission (2: 14–6: 13; 7: 2–4), and to stress the importance of the Corinthians showing their concern for the universal Church by sharing in the collection for the needy Christians in Jerusalem (8: 1–9: 15).

Ephesians

Ephesus was one of the most important towns in the Roman province of Asia, and its church was established by Paul during a two-year stay there (see Acts 18: 19–21; 19: 1–20), although an Alexandrian Jew, called Apollos, also influenced its development.

Scholars are divided over the question whether the letter was actually written by Paul, but, whilst the vocabulary is unusual, it certainly reflects Paul's teaching and draws upon his authority.

An interesting suggestion is that the letter was sent with the authority of Paul to newly established congregations to instruct them more fully on what was implied in their baptism. Some manuscripts of the letter do not contain reference to Ephesus and it is possible that it was a *circular* letter (an *encyclical*!).

Apart from the opening greeting and the closing messages, the letter can be divided into three main sections:

(i) 1: 3–23, which is fundamentally a prayer, beginning with thanksgiving for what God is and what he has done for us through Christ, and going on to include intercessory prayer on behalf of the readers;

(ii) 2: 1–3: 21, in which Paul speaks of the incorporation of the Gentiles into the one Church through the grace of God, asserts his own apostolic authority, and ends with a renewed prayer of thanksgiving;

(iii) 4: 1–6: 20, which draws out the ethical implications of Christian teaching. There is, first, a strong ecumenical note on the unity of the Church; next, a look at Christian character and family duties (where the picture of the Church as the 'bride' of Christ is introduced); and, finally, consideration of the Christian life as lived in conflict with all the forces of evil. It is only God's armour and God's weapons which enable us to battle on and gain the victory.

James

The author of this letter simply identifies himself as 'a servant of God and of the Lord Jesus Christ' (1: 1), but, from the time of Origen (AD 185–254), who came across the letter in the church at Caesarea and popularized it in Alexandria, it has been associated with James, the Lord's 'brother' or 'kinsman' who was the first bishop of Jerusalem and presided over the Jerusalem Council of AD 49 (see Acts 15: 13–21; Galatians 1: 19). Jerome, however, suggests that, whilst it may have had the authority of James, it was possibly written by someone else. The writer evidently thought in Greek, for the style is very good, and so the letter is unlikely to have been written by the 'brother of the Lord'. The letter's main theme is God's righteousness (1: 20), and it deals with this in three main sections:

(i) 1: 2–2: 26, in which there is emphasis on an authentic Christian life, as contrasted with a mere pretence;
(ii) 3: 1–18, where he considers the credentials of Christian leaders;
(iii) 4–5, in which he portrays the elements of a truly Christian character.

Whilst we speak of the 'letter' of James, it is much more like a sermon, with as many as sixty imperatives in one hundred and eight verses. It is not so much concerned with doctrine as with how a Christian ought to live. James does not take issue with Paul's emphasis on *faith*, but demands that it be a *living* faith and not merely nominal.

Hebrews

This letter, like Romans, maintains a sustained argument and helps us to see how a first-century Christian would explain his deep conviction that, in and through Christ, God has provided for us a new and living way. What he has done through Christ goes beyond all that had happened before. Christ is superior to angels and Moses. His priesthood is eternal and achieves everything which the Aaronic priesthood had failed to achieve – a clear conscience and intimate relationship with God. Jesus can save 'now and always those who come to God through him' (7: 25). The focus of the chapters is on the person of Jesus, God's son (1: 2) and yet the one who shares our humanity (2: 10–18; 4: 15–16).

The writer (we do not know who he was; Origen said 'God alone knows' who he was!) stresses that we cannot go one better on what God has himself done through Christ and so warns against turning away from the faith. By comparison with the *reality* we have in Christ, everything before (the Jewish faith and its whole sacrificial system) is nothing more than a 'shadow'. Jesus brings us to grips with the eternal, and his sacrifice on the cross is seen as his self-offering on the 'heavenly altar' – a demonstration of his perfect obedience to the Father. What he has done has an influence on everyone – at all times.

1 John

Without any personal greetings, this letter plunges straight away into a consideration of the apostolic faith (1: 1–4), which is based upon the *testimony of experience*, and ways in which the authentic character of that faith can be tested (1: 5–2: 27). The first test relates to conduct, although conduct is linked with our interpretation of reality (what God is and how we recognize him). God is goodness itself and the demand is that we should be Godlike. The second test is more theological. A Christian is a person who believes that Jesus is the Christ and that the human Jesus, whilst *truly human*, is the incarnate Son of God who perfectly shows us what the Father is like. These two tests are inextricably intertwined. Theologizing without Christian living and positive action is seen as valueless. That is why the writer goes on to consider the new life which God's children are to experience (2: 28–4: 12) and the Christian certainties which are based on love (4: 13–5: 12). The facts that 'God is love' and 'love' is experienced in action are the key to the link. It is as the Christian recognizes love as the dominant factor in his whole life, that he both experiences his free access to God and receives assurance of forgiveness through Christ.

The Psalms

From very ancient times, language in the form of poetry with musical accompaniment has been used in the liturgy of communal worship. And so there have evolved intoned poems of prayer with each one taking a traditional form according to its place in the sequence of worship. The Psalms of the Bible are poems or songs (the Greek word *psalmos* means a song) of this kind surviving from Israelite worship.

Little is known about the history of the collection of Psalms as we have it today. It is generally estimated to have been completed in the fourth century BC. The collection is in five divisions, though there are signs within these of earlier groupings. Smaller sequences of Psalms have been gathered together for various reasons. They may have been connected in liturgical usage, or belonged to the repertoire of a certain guild of Temple musicians, or they may simply have resembled one another in theme or worship. Gradually all these groups were gathered together into the present structure of the book of Psalms.

Though it is not possible to date accurately the individual Psalms, it can be deduced, both from the connection with Jerusalem and the monarchy, and from comparison with other Old Testament and extra-biblical material, that the main period of composition was in the time of the Davidic Dynasty (i.e. about 1000–587 BC). The roots of the tradition, however, go back into earlier Israelite and Canaanite worship, while its growth continues into later times.

The Psalms would normally have been composed and sung by the Temple personnel. These belonged to guilds and orders of sacred ministers, some of whom would have specialized in psalmody and music. Sometimes the kings themselves composed Psalms (David, in fact, is noted in tradition as the author of many), though it would have been more normal for the king to have had the royal prayers composed for him by a member of the Temple orders or guilds. At the very least, David was responsible for a collection of Psalms being made.

There was an appropriate type or class of composition for each situation in worship where a Psalm might be used. Themes, expressions and structure followed the convention of the types in question. Many of the present Psalms are grouped into such classes. Others, however, though having many of the traditional features, are less easily classified. Much recent and modern scholarship has been devoted to studying this classification with the result that a great deal has been added to our understanding the Psalms and their place in Israel's worship. A pioneer in this field of study was the German scholar Hermann Gunkel. By means of a classification of types, largely following the thought, mood and vocabulary in the different Psalms, Gunkel has tried to fit these Psalms into what may have been their original setting. What follows is a summary of the main categories of his classification.

Psalm types

Laments make up the largest single category of Psalms. They may be individual in character (e.g. Psalms 3, 5, 7, 13) or communal (sometimes called 'national') (e.g. Psalms 44, 74, 79). Individual laments seem to be the prayers of individual sufferers, in which there is a cry for help, a description of the sufferings or dangers encountered, and often an indication that there are enemies whom the sufferer wishes to see overthrown. There is usually an expression of confidence that God has heard the prayer and will act upon it. Regular stock images are used to describe both the plight of the sufferer and the character of the enemies at whose hand he is suffering. Communal or national laments usually incorporate cries to God to hear and come to the people's rescue. There is normally a description of the plight of the people which is intended to stir God to compassion, and a call for his judgment on their oppressors. Often there is an appeal to God's promises in the covenant he has made with Israel, and, once again, an expression of confidence that God has heard the prayer.

Thanksgiving Psalms also may be individual (e.g. Psalms 30, 32) or communal (e.g. 67, 124). Individual ones will express the kind of trouble from which the psalmist has been delivered, whilst the communal ones will refer to some particular national deliverance.

Hymns form a large class (e.g. Psalms 33, 145–150). They emphasize the element of praise, or of reverence and joy in God's presence. The reason for the call to praise and exaltation is usually given. Within this group occur the *Songs of Zion* (e.g. Psalms 46, 48) which are concerned with the Holy City, and the *Enthronement Psalms* (e.g. Psalms 47, 96–99) in which God is proclaimed King.

Royal Psalms (e.g. Psalms 2, 18, 110, 132) point to special events in the reigns of kings before the destruction of the Temple in 587 BC. There may be references to the king's enthronement, his wedding, his anniversary or some such important occurrence.

Pilgrimage Psalms (sometimes called 'gradual' Psalms) (e.g. Psalm 84, 121–134) were used by companies of pilgrims as they went up to the Temple in Jerusalem for the annual festivals.

Wisdom Psalms (e.g. Psalms 1, 73) form one of the smaller groupings and, like the Proverbs, often point to the contrasting destinies of the just and the wicked. *Torah liturgies* (as in Psalms 15 and 24) convey priestly instruction or provide liturgical dialogue, whilst *Prophetic liturgies* (as in Psalms 60 and 75) point to an oracle given by a prophet.

Alphabetical Psalms are Psalms in which each stanza begins with a consecutive letter of the Hebrew alphabet. The most impressive example is Psalm 119; in every stanza the first letter of each verse is the same, and there are twenty-two stanzas, one for each letter of the Hebrew alphabet. Psalms 111 and 145 are simpler examples.

The numbering of the Psalms

The numbering in this book's commentary and articles follows that which is used in most modern Bible translations. Liturgical books have tended to follow the numbering of the Septuagint (the Greek translation of the Old Testament). There, because some Psalms were merged (9 and 10) and another divided (147), a scheme arose which differed from that of the Hebrew Bible. For most of the psalter (11–146) the Hebrew counting is one ahead of the Greek; also, Psalms 114–116 are differently divided.

Hebrew	Septuagint and Vulgate
1–8	1–8
9–10	9
11–113	10–112

13

Hebrew	Septuagint and Vulgate
114–115	113
116	114–115
117–146	116–145
147	146–147
148–150	148–150

The Responsorial Psalms are printed out in full in this book, not only for ease of reference, but to provide groups and individuals with material for their prayerful response to the readings. (The Greek or liturgical number of the Psalm is given in brackets after the usual biblical one.)

Seasons I

ADVENT

Liturgical Introduction

Advent is a season of mixed origins, as a consequence of which it has long been far from clear whether it is primarily concerned with the first or with the second coming of Christ. The new Roman calendar states firmly that it is concerned with both, and with both as they are related one to the other: 'The season of Advent has a double character: for it is a time of preparing for the solemnity of the Nativity, in which is recalled the first coming of the Son of God to men; and at the same time it is the season in which, *by this recalling*, our minds are led to look for the second coming of Christ at the end of time. On both these counts, Advent is to be seen as a time of devout and joyful expectancy' (*Calendarium Romanum, Notae*, 39; italics ours).

The second coming of Christ our Lord 'in glory to judge the living and the dead' (Creed) is proposed as an object of our *joyful* expectancy, an object of longing and hope; not, as so often has been the case in the past, of terror and of dread. We must indeed prepare ourselves for it, with the true repentance of a humble spirit and a contrite heart; the call to be always prepared is in the Gospel of the first Sunday; the Baptist's call to repent is in the Gospel of the second Sunday; but in both that and the Gospel of the third Sunday the emphasis is on 'preparing the way of the Lord', and on who that Lord is: it is to *him* that we must look, and in such a way that he 'may find an eager welcome at his coming and call us to his side in the kingdom of heaven' (Collect, first Sunday).

On the fourth Sunday, and on weekdays from 17 December, all the emphasis is on the forthcoming feast of the Nativity. But the purpose of our celebrating it is summed up in the Preface for this period:

> In his love Christ has filled us with joy,
> as we prepare to celebrate his birth,
> so that when he comes he may find us watching in prayer,
> our hearts filled with wonder and praise.

First Sunday of Advent

First Reading   Isaiah 63: 16–17; 64: 1, 3–8

A reading taken from the chapters ascribed to the Third or Trito-Isaiah. Possibly written in the last quarter of the sixth century BC it reflects some of the frustration and tension of the post-exilic period, but also echoes the confidence of the Second Isaiah in God's saving power and acts as a constant recall of the people to their covenant allegiance. The passage is part of a long psalm of lament and entreaty, 63: 7–64: 11, all of which gives added depth to the selection. The basis of confidence is a recalling of God's saving acts of election and covenant, and the recognition of the fatherhood of God. Notice the twice-repeated 'Lord, you are our Father'. The very faithfulness of God highlights the sinfulness of the people and the expression of penitence becomes an urgent appeal to the Lord for mercy and grace. The movement from confession of guilt to confidence marked by the decisive 'and yet' is typical of the lament Psalms and illustrates the constant experience of God as redeemer.

Responsorial Psalm   80 (79)

℞ *God of hosts, bring us back;*
   let your face shine on us and we shall be saved.

1 O shepherd of Israel, hear us,
   shine forth from your cherubim throne.
   O Lord, rouse up your might,
   O Lord, come to our help. (R)

2 God of hosts, turn again, we implore,
   look down from heaven and see.
   Visit this vine and protect it,
   the vine your right hand has planted. (R)

3 May your hand be on the man you have chosen,
   the man you have given your strength.
   And we shall never forsake you again:
   give us life that we may call upon your name. (R)

This Psalm is part of a national lament (cf. p. 12), evoking by the powerful metaphors of shepherd and vine the relationship of God

18

with his people; from this follows the certainty that the prayer of the refrain, taking up the Aaronic blessing of Numbers 6: 24ff., will be heard.

Second Reading   **1 Corinthians 1: 3–9**

The Corinthian community, reflected in the Pauline letters, was exuberant and turbulent; Paul had to modify its boasting and censure its quarrelling and divisions. The opening of this letter is a typical Pauline greeting and thanksgiving that sounds a positive note for what is to follow. God's initiative is at work among them by his Spirit and he remains faithful to his gift, but the Corinthians have to recognize that their stance must be one of alert expectancy; they have not arrived, but are waiting for the full realization of God's kingdom in the *parousia*, the second coming of Jesus Christ. The last line of the reading underlines the reality of the Christian fellowship, or community, the context in which God's gifts operate.

Gospel   **Mark 13: 33–37**

Chapter 13 of Mark's Gospel is a discourse stressing the culmination of the end-times and the coming in glory of the Son of Man. The early Christian community, living in a situation of persecution, was very conscious of the Second Coming and this conviction gave them hope in their distress and assured them of the victory already attained by Christ. But the conviction should lead not to complacency but to prayerful alertness. This is stressed in today's reading which concludes the discourse and reminds all Christians in every age that 'being on guard' and 'watching' are keynotes of the Christian life. Some ancient manuscripts add 'pray' (cf. RSV reading) to the other two imperatives of the passage. Advent is a recalling of the first coming and preparation for the second.

Second Sunday of Advent

Prepare the way of the Lord!

First Reading   Isaiah 40: 1–5, 9–11

Chapters 40–55 are ascribed to Second Isaiah, who was writing about 540 BC when the Babylonian power was declining and Cyrus of Persia was gaining ascendancy. This is the Cyrus whom Second Isaiah calls the Messiah, the Lord's anointed one (45: 1), because through him Israel is to gain restoration. Second Isaiah addresses the Israelite exiles in Babylon with a message of joyful hope, well illustrated in this passage, which opens the 'Book of Consolation' as it is sometimes called. The imperatives underline the nearness of salvation and the language is expressive of a new Exodus, a favourite theme of Second Isaiah. The journey through the wilderness is described as a triumphant royal march, reminiscent of the pageantry that the Israelites witnessed in Babylon. Although at the time of writing Jerusalem was still in ruins, the confident hope of the prophet sees the victorious presence of God in his city. The last verse is rich in the imagery so typical of Second Isaiah.

Responsorial Psalm   85 (84)

℟ *Let us see, O Lord, your mercy*
and give us your saving help.

1 I will hear what the Lord God has to say,
   a voice that speaks of peace,
   peace for his people.
   His help is near for those who fear him
   and his glory will dwell in our land. (R)

2 Mercy and faithfulness have met;
   justice and peace have embraced.
   Faithfulness shall spring from the earth
   and justice look down from heaven. (R)

3 The Lord will make us prosper
   and our earth shall yield its fruit.
   Justice shall march before him
   and peace shall follow his steps. (R)

The last part of a Psalm of national lament that seems to herald the return from exile in language similar to Second Isaiah. This section is a prophetic word of comfort, that appears to be a reply to the lament.

Second Reading   2 Peter 3: 8–14

Although attributed to Peter, this letter is probably a much later work belonging to the second century AD and possibly the latest work of the New Testament. As time passes hope in the *parousia* has to be reiterated, and the fact that Christians are people pledged to wait on the Day of the Lord and so have here 'no abiding city' has to be emphasized. This waiting does not result in apathy but actually gives an urgency to the quality of life. The apocalyptic verses of the passage echo much of the thought of earlier New Testament writings.

Gospel   Mark 1: 1–8

The first verse of this Gospel is Mark's prologue in which he clearly states his aim. He is proclaiming the good news, the gospel (it is the same word) of Jesus Christ, and he places this in the context of the expectancy shown in the Old Testament. He indicates the link by quoting from Malachi 3: 1 and Isaiah 40: 3 (the same passage used as the first reading). And it is against this background that Mark's Gospel must be read, as a realization of the fulfilment of God's plan in Jesus Christ. This is shown further by Mark's presentation of John the Baptist as another Elijah (cf. 2 Kings 1: 8), which indicates the fulfilment of another expectation in Malachi 4: 5. The New Age is coming in Jesus Christ as John the Baptist asserts by saying that Jesus will baptize with the Holy Spirit, for the outpouring of the Spirit was expected to occur in the last age (see Joel 2: 28f.). This passage, therefore, reminds its readers in the early Christian community that they must show the same expectancy and follow John the Baptist's injunction to repent. Only in this way could they prepare for the Second Coming.

Third Sunday of Advent

Exulting for joy in the Lord.

First Reading   Isaiah 61: 1–2, 10–11

Although taken from Third Isaiah (56–66) this passage reflects the references in Second Isaiah (40–55) to God's Servant. These passages all emphasize the saving power of God exercised through his servant. In 61: 1–9 the writer builds up an ideal picture of the final age with striking contrasts between before and after. In Luke's Gospel this passage is used by Jesus as virtually a charter of his mission (Luke 4: 16–22); here the new age is breaking in in Jesus Christ. In the sixth century BC the vision of the new age is an encouragement to the returned exiles faced with ruin and tension. Before the vision the prophet breaks into a typical psalm of praise and thanksgiving (61: 10–11) concluding with a note of certain trust in God's power.

Responsorial Psalm   Luke 1: 46–50, 53–54

℟ *My soul rejoices in my God.*

1 My soul glorifies the Lord,
   my spirit rejoices in God, my Saviour.
   He looks on his servant in her nothingness;
   henceforth all ages will call me blessed. (R)

2 The Almighty works marvels for me.
   Holy his name!
   His mercy is from age to age,
   on those who fear him. (R)

3 He fills the starving with good things,
   sends the rich away empty.
   He protects Israel, his servant,
   remembering his mercy. (R)

One of the hymns of Luke's Infancy Narrative, proclaimed by Mary when she visited her cousin Elizabeth. It follows closely not only the form but also the content of some hymns of the Old Testament (see Hannah's song in 1 Samuel 2: 1–10). Like the first reading, it gets its effect by contrast. Luke interweaves Old Testament material into his song to show how the Old Testament has been fulfilled in Christ.

Second Reading   **1 Thessalonians 5: 16–24**

Thessalonians is possibly the earliest of the New Testament works, being a letter written by Paul from Corinth about AD 51. The Thessalonians were worried about the timing of the *parousia*, the Second Coming, and about those who died before it happened. This information had been brought to Paul by Timothy (1 Thessalonians 3: 6) and Paul hastens to reassure the young community, emphasizing what should be the attitude of those waiting for the Lord. Thankful for what God has done for them in Christ, their lives should reflect their response. This passage is the conclusion of the letter and is typical of Paul. The short injunctions give us a glimpse into the life of the early Christian community. Christianity is a whole way of life based on the certainty of God's saving power in Christ. The reason for the choice of this reading for Advent and the relevance of its message are obvious.

Gospel   **John 1: 6–8, 19–28**

John's Gospel was the last to be written, the final editing possibly taking place at the end of the first century AD and its distinctive emphasis shows the fruit of reflection on the mystery of Christ. Some scholars see the whole Gospel as a judicial enquiry, culminating in the final trial of the Passion, with the witnesses of the light and the darkness. John presents the Baptist with the emphasis on witness rather than either fore-runner or baptizer. In fact so strong is this emphasis that in the dialogue the Baptist is seen as repudiating the role of Elijah attributed to him by the other Gospels. He was 'a witness to speak for the light'. The first part of the passage is taken from the prologue and placed in this context so that the importance of John as witness to the light is shown. This theme of the witness of the Baptist appears elsewhere in the Gospel e.g. – 1: 29–34, 3: 22–30, 5: 33–36, 10: 40–41. As an Advent reading it continues to give witness to the light, a light that 'darkness has not overcome' (John 1: 5).

Fourth Sunday of Advent

The Lord is faithful to his promise and his love lasts for ever.

First Reading   **2 Samuel 7: 1–5, 8–11, 16**

The Deuteronomic history, possibly prefaced by Deuteronomy and stretching from Joshua to 2 Kings, was compiled from older sources and edited at the time of the Babylonian Exile in the sixth century BC when Israel's national hopes were shattered. It is expressive of a complete conviction of God's saving power operative in Israel's history. The prophecy of Nathan, one of the key Deuteronomic texts, forms the basis of today's reading. David, having defeated the Philistines, captured Jerusalem and established the Ark in that city, determined to build a house fitting for the Lord. But the Lord, through Nathan, made it clear that this was not to be, but that he, the Lord, would build a house, a dynasty, for David. This text is important in the development of messianic and 'Son of David' hopes.

Responsorial Psalm   **89 (88)**

℟ *I will sing for ever of your love, O Lord.*

1 I will sing for ever of your love, O Lord;
   through all ages my mouth will proclaim your truth.
   Of this I am sure, that your love lasts for ever,
   that your truth is firmly established as the heavens. (R)

2 'I have made a covenant with my chosen one;
   I have sworn to David my servant:
   I will establish your dynasty for ever
   and set up your throne through all ages.' (R)

3 He will say to me: 'You are my father,
   my God, the rock who saves me.'
   I will keep my love for him always;
   for him my covenant shall endure. (R)

A selection of verses from Psalm 89, a hymn of praise (see p. 12). The whole Psalm is a reflection on the Lord's covenant loyalty and reiterates, indeed appears to quote from, 2 Samuel 7, our first reading.

Second Reading   **Romans 16: 25–27**

Romans is possibly the last writing of Paul and it is his testament to the heart of the Christian message. Addressed to a community he had not visited and not dealing with any specific problem, it contains his mature reflection on the good news. The reading is the doxology that concludes the letter. Although the authenticity of this conclusion is disputed, it nevertheless forms a fitting meditation on the ways of the eternal God and so forms a link between the first and third readings, both of which illumine the working of God's plan.

Gospel   **Luke 1: 26–38**

The early Christian community reflected on God's saving power in Christ in the light of the Scriptures and Luke's Infancy Narrative (Luke 1 and 2) is a magnificent example of this meditation. Although it does not contain any actual quotations it is a tapestry of Old Testament allusions. Today's reading is a good example of this and some of the richness of these allusions is brought home because of its juxtaposition with 2 Samuel 7. In this annunciation scene Mary stands as the very epitome of Israel, but a faithful Israel ready to listen to the Lord. The stress on Mary's virginity takes an added dimension when seen in terms of the virgin Israel (see e.g. Amos 5: 2). The presence of the Spirit and the Power of the Most High points to the new creation. The name Jesus ('Joshua' in the Old Testament) means 'saviour'. In the Bible names are significant. Luke in his Gospel is to stress Christ's saving power and this is the *good news* that Christmas celebrates.

CHRISTMAS DAY

Midnight Mass

Today a Saviour has been born to you!

First Reading   Isaiah 9: 1–7

The first Isaiah (1–39) was writing in the tiny southern kingdom of
Judah from 742 to beyond 701 BC, at a time when that kingdom was
under constant threat not only from the growing power of Assyria
but also from the intrigues of the northern kingdom of Israel. The
material shows constant signs of re-editing by which the followers of
Isaiah underlined and drew out his message for another age. This
passage, a psalm of thanksgiving, celebrates either the birth of a son
to the king or the accession of the king, and is typical of the
theological understanding of kingship that developed in Israel. It is a
clarion call of hope and trust when the outward situation did not
seem to warrant this. An ideal picture with vivid strokes of contrast,
it became a favourite for Christians as they proclaimed that these
hopes had been realized in the birth of Jesus Christ.

Responsorial Psalm   96 (95)

℟ *Today a saviour has been born to us;*
  he is Christ the Lord.

1 O sing a new song to the Lord,
   sing to the Lord all the earth.
   O sing to the Lord, bless his name. (R)

2 Proclaim his help day by day,
   tell among the nations his glory
   and his wonders among all the peoples. (R)

3 Let the heavens rejoice and earth be glad,
   let the sea and all within it thunder praise,
   let the land and all it bears rejoice,
   all the trees of the wood shout for joy
   at the presence of the Lord for he comes,
   he comes to rule the earth. (R)

4 With justice he will rule the world,
  he will judge the peoples with his truth. (R)

A royal Psalm (cf. p. 13), it celebrates the kingship of the Lord, and the use of the response from Luke 2: 11 indicates that this kingship was made visible in Jesus Christ. This Psalm was also used in 1 Chronicles 16 to celebrate the arrival of the Ark of the Covenant in Jerusalem.

Second Reading   **Titus 2: 11–14**

One of the Pastoral Letters, possibly compiled early in the second century AD and attributed to Paul, Titus brings out the challenge of the Incarnation to every aspect of life. The use of the word 'appearing' which is also the basis of 'epiphany' in Greek, links the first and second coming, the word being used for both. The movement towards fulfilment is emphasized in the last sentence, full of Old Testament allusions (e.g. Exodus 19: 5; Deuteronomy 14: 2) which sees the Church as the New Israel. The 'has been revealed' and 'we are waiting' bring out the two levels present in Advent and Christmas – the *now* and the *not yet*; this is the tension that gives a rich urgency to Christian living.

Gospel   **Luke 2: 1–14**

The theme of kingship is taken up and stressed in this section of Luke's Infancy Narrative with its reiterated use of David's name. This is Luke's way of showing the fulfilment of Israel's hopes in Jesus Christ. The precise date of the census has been considerably debated, but Luke's main interest is to place the birth of Jesus in the context of world history. The reference to the manger and shepherds could well be a link with David, the shepherd-king. At the same time we have Luke's characteristic emphasis on God's favouring of the lowly. It is they who are the first recipients of the good news. In the angels' message we have a summary of all the major themes of Luke's writing – Jesus is central; he is the Saviour; the humble welcome him; the overwhelming note of joy is present throughout. The verb, translated 'bring you news', is the verbal form of 'good news', 'gospel'. Christmas is gospel.

Dawn Mass

Glory to God in the highest – The Lord is born for us!

First Reading   **Isaiah 62: 11–12**

These verses conclude the section 60: 1–62: 12 of the Third Isaiah glorying in the coming of the new age, visualized as a restoration of Jerusalem and of God's presence in his city. A reading of the whole section brings out the reason for its use in the Christmas liturgy. The saviour's coming is depicted as a victorious, triumphant procession to Zion. Names and renaming are very important in the Old Testament. So here we have four new names given – two recalling the experience of salvation at the time of the Exodus and two speaking of Jerusalem (= Zion), David's city as God's chosen dwelling-place. (We find this same emphasis on *new* names in Hosea 1: 6, 9; 2: 23.) The proclamation is not only to Israel but 'to the ends of the earth'.

Responsorial Psalm   **97 (96)**

℟ *This day new light will shine upon the earth:
the Lord is born for us.*

1 The Lord is king, let earth rejoice,
   the many coastlands be glad.
   The skies proclaim his justice;
   all peoples see his glory. (R)

2 Light shines forth for the just
   and joy for the upright of heart.
   Rejoice, you just, in the Lord;
   give glory to his holy name. (R)

A Royal Psalm (cf. p. 13) celebrating the kingship of the Lord, its application to Christmas is shown by the response. The first verse is a summons to the whole universe and its inhabitants, echoing the first reading.

Second Reading   **Titus 3: 4–7**

Throughout the Bible the saving act of God is always presented as a gratuitous act on God's part; the initiative rests with him. In this

28

reading from Titus the saving love of God is seen as 'poured over us through Jesus Christ our saviour'. This is expressed, too, in the language of baptism with its dual action of cleansing and renewal in the Holy Spirit. 'Poured out' (with its allusion to Joel 2: 28) and the last sentence of our passage bring out the inauguration of the last days in Jesus Christ. Once again we can see the link between the Advent theme and Christmas.

Gospel   **Luke 2: 15–20**

This section ends the account of the shepherds episode in Luke's Infancy Narrative, and illustrates his consummate skill as a story-teller. The verbs of response bring out the overwhelming effect of the event hymned by the angels. The shepherds 'hurry away', the same verb used of Mary after the annunciation (Luke 1: 39). The onlookers were 'astonished' (RSV 'wondered'), a word used to describe the reaction in face of revelation. By contrast Mary 'pondered'; she entered into the inner meaning of this revelation. Finally, in language typical of Luke, the shepherds are said to 'glorify and praise'. The whole of Luke's Infancy Narrative is permeated with this sense of joy and the human response of praise. After all, it is a fitting response to the good news of Christmas – the Lord is born for us!

Day Mass

The Word was made flesh.

First Reading   **Isaiah 52: 7–10**

The Second Isaiah writing about 540 BC calls the people to rejoice in the hope of their deliverance, their salvation. Verses 3–6 have painted a picture of the nation in captivity that serves to highlight their salvation. Both these verses and verses 11–12 which follow our passage have allusions to the Exodus from Egypt and so the return of the people to Zion (= Jerusalem) is seen as a New Exodus. The Exodus is the event in Israel's history which focuses on salvation, and this new expression of it is to be hymned to the ends of the earth. We have an echo of the last verse of this passage in Luke 2: 31.

Responsorial Psalm   98 (97)

℞ *All the ends of the earth have seen*
the salvation of our God.

1 Sing a new song to the Lord
   for he has worked wonders.
   His right hand and his holy arm
   have brought salvation. (R)

2 The Lord has made known his salvation;
   has shown his justice to the nations.
   He has remembered his truth and love
   For the house of Israel. (R)

3 All the ends of the earth have seen
   the salvation of our God.
   Shout to the Lord all the earth,
   ring out your joy. (R)

4 Sings psalms to the Lord with the harp,
   with the sound of music.
   With trumpets and the sound of the horn
   acclaim the King the Lord. (R)

The first reading is taken up by this hymn of praise (cf. p. 12) for the deliverance which the Lord has worked for his people. The terms 'truth and love' are expressions of the Lord's covenant-loyalty and are often translated 'faithfulness and steadfast love'.

Second Reading   **Hebrews 1: 1–6**

The Christian conviction of the fulfilment of all things in Christ is vividly brought out in the opening of the letter to the Hebrews by an unknown author. The stress throughout this letter is that by, through and with Jesus Christ we obtain access to God. The author has a strong sense of the exaltation of Jesus and of his eternal intercession (7: 25). Verse 3 seems to take up the praise applied to wisdom in the Book of Wisdom 7: 22–30. In the early Church they used this passage to understand Jesus Christ. He is seen as the

Wisdom of God. As wisdom was seen as God's agent in creation, so, too, is Christ. This theme is taken up and developed in our Gospel reading.

Gospel   **John 1: 1-18**

Ecclesiasticus or Sirach 24, Wisdom 7: 22–30, Proverbs 8: 22–31 can all help in the understanding of the beautiful prologue of John's Gospel which is a mature reflection on the meaning of the Incarnation. The great struggle between light and darkness (a constant theme of John) is introduced here (cf. John 12: 31–36), but with the utter conviction that it is 'a light that darkness has not overcome'. The two references to John the Baptist in the prologue, possibly later insertions in an already-existing hymn, brings out another major theme of the Gospel, that of witness. The Gospel brings together two important and yet contrasting words – 'word' and 'flesh'. 'Word' points to the power and transcendence of God; 'flesh' to man in all his weakness and frailty. And yet the two are joined together in the incarnation. The full revelation of God is spoken to us through his Son (Hebrews 1: 1). 'It is the only Son, who is nearest to the Father's heart, who has made him known' (John 1: 18).

Holy Family (Sunday in Christmas Octave)

'Honour your father and your mother' (Exodus 20: 12).

First Reading   **Ecclesiasticus 3: 2–6, 12–14**

Ecclesiasticus or Sirach survives in the Greek translation of the Old Testament and is not in the Hebrew Bible. It was translated about 132 BC by the grandson of Jesus the Son of Sirach who wrote it in Hebrew. It belongs to the Wisdom literature and it reflects a search for the wise action in all man's dealings. Wisdom does not have an intellectual emphasis, but refers to integrity of life. 'To fear the Lord is the root of wisdom and her branches are long life' (Ecclesiasticus 1: 20). The right relationship between God and man ensures the right relationship between man and man, here illustrated in the context of the family. (This passage could be a commentary on Exodus 20: 12.)

Responsorial Psalm   **128 (127)**

℟ *O blessed are those who fear the Lord*
   and walk in his ways!

1 O blessed are those who fear the Lord
  and walk in his ways!
  By the labour of your hands you shall eat.
  You will be happy and prosper. (R)

2 Your wife like a fruitful vine
  in the heart of your house;
  your children like shoots of the olive,
  around your table. (R)

3 Indeed this shall be blessed
  the man who fears the Lord.
  May the Lord bless you from Zion
  all the days of your life! (R)

A Wisdom Psalm (cf. p. 13), opening with a beatitude and showing how a life of integrity overflows into the blessing of family and work.

Second Reading   **Colossians 3: 12–21**

This passage comes from the second part of Paul's letter to the Colossians, one of his later letters, in which he moves into exhortation. Many of the injunctions are homely, as was found in Ecclesiasticus, but the motivation that gives the exhortation strength is clearly presented. You are 'God's chosen race' and you must let 'the peace of Christ reign in your hearts'. Notice the number of imperatives and the many areas of life covered. It gives a vivid picture of the struggle of an early Christian community which is encouraged to realize the ideal of a community truly living 'in Christ'. Colossians 3: 18–4: 1 is based on the common 'household code' of the Stoic society, but it is used by Paul with the constantly repeated 'Lord' – seven times in eight verses.

Gospel   **Luke 2: 22–40**

All the readings for today have centred on family relationships and this is further illustrated by this passage taken from Luke's Infancy Narrative. Every participant is presented as attentive and receptive to the Lord, representative of pious Israel. In the context of fulfilling the Law, Mary and Joseph hear the future of their son. This is expressed in the canticle of Simeon, the last of the beautiful hymns in this narrative, and adopted by the Church as the canticle for her Night Prayer. Again fulfilment is stressed by numerous Old Testament allusions. The way of the cross is already present and Mary's own involvement in her son's suffering is indicated. In the detailed characterization of Anna we can see Luke's deep interest in the part played by women. Also the presence of a second witness fulfils the prescription of Deuteronomy 19: 15. The passage ends with a pointer to the ideal family – caring parents and an obedient child whose growth and development are not stunted.

Mary, Mother of God (1st January)

God sent his Son, born of a woman.

First Reading   **Numbers 6: 22–27**

The book of Numbers is a reflection on the Sinai and Wilderness experience. The first chapters are a great roll-call of the nation, with special reference to the position of the priests and Levites. This section ends with the beautiful blessing of Aaron, that formed part of the later Temple service and became the concluding prayer of the Jewish Sabbath morning service. A prayer familiar to Jesus, it is used by Christians to express their realization of God's saving act in his Son, God's supreme blessing for all mankind.

Responsorial Psalm   **67 (66)**

℟ *O God, be gracious and bless us.*

1 God, be gracious and bless us
   and let your face shed its light upon us.
   So will your ways be known upon earth
   and all nations learn your saving help. (R)

2 Let the nations be glad and exult
   for you rule the world with justice.
   With fairness you rule the peoples,
   you guide the nations on earth. (R)

3 Let the peoples praise you, O God;
   let all the peoples praise you.
   May God still give us his blessing
   till the ends of the earth revere him. (R)

This Psalm calling down God's blessing on the whole earth echoes the first reading. It is also a Psalm of Thanksgiving (cf. p. 12) recognizing God's salvation at work.

Second Reading   **Galatians 4: 4–7**

Paul was impatient with the Galatians because they appeared to be underestimating the power of God's saving act in Christ by turning again to the prescriptions of the Law. He boldly asserts that Christ has taken on the very curse of the Law in order to free all from slavery to the Law, and to give them the grace of the Spirit that enables them to say 'Abba, Father'. They are sons not slaves. The very use of the Aramaic *Abba* would recall the tradition of Jesus' own prayer, for *Abba* is the affectionate way of addressing a father. This closely packed passage is a reflection on the meaning of Christ's coming. This coming was at the appointed time, the time of fulfilment. Although Mary is not mentioned by name, the assertion that this fulfilment came about by Jesus being 'born of a woman' and the use of this reading for this feast day, highlights Mary's place in God's plan of salvation.

Gospel   **Luke 2: 16–21**

The Gospel continues with Luke's beautiful Infancy Narrative, a favourite of the Christmas season. As Mary had hurried to her cousin Elizabeth after the angel's message, so the shepherds hurried to Bethlehem. The scene appears simple but is very carefully constructed to bring out the importance of the event. We are given three reactions to the incident. The hearers are astonished, and this astonishment conveys the sense of wonder in the presence of God's revelation. Mary 'treasured and pondered', expressing her constant receptiveness. The shepherds 'glorified and praised'; this 'praise' is a recurring theme in Luke's Gospel. It is also closely linked with joy – which is dominant in Luke's account. The story ends with the naming of the baby and the significance of the name is stressed: 'the name the angel had given him before his conception' – the name that means 'saviour'.

Second Sunday after Christmas

God chose us in Christ.

First Reading   **Ecclesiasticus 24: 1–2, 8–12**

As we have seen, Ecclesiasticus belongs to the Greek translation of the Jewish Bible and does not occur in the Hebrew collection. The whole of chapter 24 from which our passage is taken is a hymn in praise of Wisdom. Wisdom is personified and is seen very much as God's mediator in his creation and in his dealings with his people. Indeed in verse 23 the author equates Wisdom and the Law. Much of this thought was picked up in the New Testament and used to express the role of Christ. This is illustrated in the Gospel passage of today.

Responsorial Psalm   **147**

℟ *The Word was made flesh,*
  and lived among us.
  or *Alleluia!*

1 O praise the Lord, Jerusalem!
  Zion, praise your God!
  He has strengthened the bars of your gates,
  he has blessed the children within you. (R)

2 He established peace on your borders,
  he feeds you with finest wheat.
  He sends out his word to the earth
  and swiftly runs his command. (R)

3 He makes his word known to Jacob,
  to Israel his laws and decrees.
  He has not dealt thus with other nations;
  he has not taught them his decrees.
  Alleluia! (R)

A hymn of praise (cf. p. 12) which brings out Yahweh's care for his people, here symbolized as Zion. The response, taken from the Gospel, sees that care exemplified in the Father sending his Son to dwell with his people.

Second Reading   **Ephesians 1: 3–6, 15–18**

It is worth reading the whole of verses 3–14, a beautiful hymn which extols God's plan of salvation, in order to get the setting of our passage. The writer, in thinking of the salvation given by God through Christ and of the Ephesians sharing in this salvation, sees here the grounds for thanksgiving. He also prays that the Ephesians will appreciate in their lives the full meaning of God's gift. It is to affect the whole life of the Church. In this epistle we have the identification of the Church with the body of Christ.

Gospel   **John 1: 1–18**

This is the famous prologue of John's Gospel that has already been used in the Christmas season. The Wisdom aspect is highlighted by using it in conjunction with Ecclesiasticus 24. As Wisdom was seen as taking up her abode – indeed 'pitching her tent' – in Israel – so is the 'Word made flesh' and 'pitches his tent among us'. (The Greek word used for 'dwell' literally refers to 'pitching a tent'.) But 'his own people did not accept him' – the sense of division that leads ultimately to the Cross even finds a place here. But nothing can overcome the light and the revelation of the Father through the Son is assured, as the last verses make clear.

Epiphany (6th January, or Sunday between 2nd and 8th)

We saw his star as it rose and have come to do the Lord homage.

First Reading   **Isaiah 60: 1–6**

Although this passage comes from the Third Isaiah (56–66), chapters 60–62 reflect the vibrant confidence of the Second Isaiah; at the dawning of a new age seen in the ending of the Babylonian exile. The presence of the Lord is again in Jerusalem; he is a light that will draw all nations. The scattered members of the Jewish community are to be brought back as sons and daughters to a rejoicing mother. The richness of the scene is vividly painted in verse 6 and it is imagery such as this that has helped to fill out popular narrative details for the feast of the Epiphany. Essentially the feast celebrates the drawing of all peoples to Christ.

Responsorial Psalm   72 (71)

℟ *All nations shall fall prostrate before you, O Lord.*

1 O God, give your judgement to the king,
   to a king's son your justice,

that he may judge your people in justice
and your poor in right judgement. (R)

2 In his days justice shall flourish
and peace till the moon fails.
He shall rule from sea to sea,
from the Great River to earth's bounds. (R)

3 The kings of Tarshish and the sea coasts
shall pay him tribute.
The kings of Sheba and Seba
shall bring him gifts.
Before him all kings shall fall prostrate,
all nations shall serve him. (R)

4 For he shall save the poor when they cry
and the needy who are helpless.
He will have pity on the weak
and save the lives of the poor. (R)

A royal Psalm (cf. p. 13). Although possibly used at the enthrone-ment of the king, it came to have messianic overtones, pointing to an ideal situation when the king will rule over an extensive empire, and receive tribute from East and West. This could be an allusion to Solomon's glory, but used in today's feast, it points to the glory of Christ.

Second Reading   **Ephesians 3: 2–3, 5–6**

This letter emphasizes the reconciliation of Jews and Gentiles in Christ. To read 2: 11–22 gives further depth to our passage. The feast of the Epiphany – or 'manifestation' or 'revelation', as the word means – highlights this proclamation of the good news to the pagan or Gentile. What is proclaimed is the gospel of peace, 'peace to you who were far away and peace to those who were near at hand' (Ephesians 2: 17; Isaiah 57: 19).

Gospel   **Matthew 2: 1–12**

We read now Matthew's Infancy Narrative in the light of our two previous passages; Christ is seen as drawing all, including the Gen-tiles, to himself. The Gentiles are symbolized by the wise men. The kingship of Christ is brought out; it has already been asserted that he was son of David (1: 1) and this is re-emphasized by placing his birth in Bethlehem, David's city. The quotation is from the prophet Micah (5: 2f.) writing at a time when Judah was being attacked by Sennacherib, King of Assyria, about 700 BC. The future king will inaugurate the new era of glory and peace. The use of the quotation here develops the theme of Christ's kingship, contrasted with that of Herod. Tradition has embellished the story, turning the wise men into three kings and giving symbolic value to their gifts, but the story still asserts the Epiphany (manifestation) of Christ to all nations.

Baptism of the Lord (Sunday after 6th January)

You are my Son, the Beloved; my favour rests on you.

First Reading   **Isaiah 42: 1–4, 6–7**

This is the first of the four so-called *servant songs* (42: 1–4; 49: 1–6; 50: 4–9; 52: 13–53: 12) we find in the Second Isaiah. Reflections on these songs in the early Christian community resulted in their application to Christ's ministry and death. Read together they depict the beloved of God who works solely to realize God's plan and who, by his work and suffering, brings healing (i.e. salvation) to all. This song is echoed in the narrative of Jesus' baptism, but it is the movement behind all the songs that needs to be kept in mind. We do not know to whom the songs refer. (Some see them as referring to the prophet himself, others as a personification of Israel, others as the ideal righteous sufferer.) Written towards the end of the Babylonian exile near the end of the sixth century BC, the passage reflects on that longing for restoration that would be a new exodus and a new conquest. Most of the language of the Second Isaiah portrays an ideal, and its use in relation to Jesus Christ portrays the realization of that ideal.

Responsorial Psalm   **29 (28)**

℞ *The Lord will bless his people with peace.*

1 O give the Lord you sons of God,
   give the Lord glory and power;
   give the Lord the glory of his name.
   Adore the Lord in his holy court. (R)

2 The Lord's voice resounding on the waters,
   the Lord on the immensity of waters;
   the voice of the Lord, full of power,
   the voice of the Lord, full of splendour. (R)

3 The God of glory thunders.
   In his temple they all cry: 'Glory!'
   The Lord sat enthroned over the flood;
   the Lord sits as king for ever. (R)

A hymn (cf. p. 12) in praise of the greatness and power of Yahweh.
The repeated use of the phrase 'the voice of Yahweh' (seven times in
the complete Psalm) might have motivated its choice for today's
feast.

Second Reading   **Acts 10: 34–38**

The conversion of Cornelius and his household marked the entry of
the Gentiles into the Christian community. Sometimes Peter's
speech (10: 34–43) is seen as a miniature Gospel and here is stressed
the start of Jesus' ministry after 'God had anointed him with the
Holy Spirit and with power'. The same Holy Spirit comes down on
Cornelius and his household and leads to their baptism by Peter.
The emphasis of today's liturgy is on beginnings.

Gospel   **Mark 1: 7–11**

Mark has no Infancy Narrative but plunges straight into John the
Baptist's ministry and Jesus appears on the scene without introduction or warning. The effect is dramatic, and the dramatic is a
characteristic of Mark's Gospel. In fact, in contrast to the other
evangelists, his account of the Baptism of Jesus is stark and the
words forceful; notice 'the heavens torn apart'. The effect is to place

the emphasis on God's action and the voice from heaven. The symbolism of the dove is not clear, but this vivid indication of the Spirit is the sign of the new age, the breaking in of the end-time. Finally the words echo both Isaiah 42: 1 (see first reading) and Psalm 2: 7, a royal Psalm that was interpreted of the Messiah and became a favourite of the early Christian community. Mark starts his Gospel with 'The beginning of the gospel of Jesus Christ Son of God' and the baptism reinforces this.

(Next Sunday's readings are on p. 95)

Note on Sundays in Ordinary Time

The first Sunday in Ordinary Time is always the feast of the Baptism of the Lord. The other Sundays then follow until Lent supervenes; the sequence begins again on the Sunday after Trinity Sunday. However, the sequence does not recommence exactly where it left off. (This gives the flexibility essential because years vary in their number of Sundays and in the position of Easter.) Either two or three Sundays are omitted in any one year. The table shows which these will be.

Sundays in Ordinary Time

Years	5	6	7	8	9	10	11
1982	7 Feb	14 Feb	21 Feb	—	—	—	13 Jun
1985	10 Feb	17 Feb	—	—	—	9 Jun	16 Jun
1988	7 Feb	14 Feb	—	—	—	5 Jun	12 Jun
1991	10 Feb	—	—	—	2 Jun	9 Jun	16 Jun
1994	6 Feb	13 Feb	—	—	—	5 Jun	12 Jun

Seasons II

LENT

Liturgical Introduction

Lent is a time of rebirth and renewal for the whole Church, 'for both the catechumens and the faithful are prepared for the celebration of the paschal mystery by the Lenten liturgy: the catechumens by the various stages of Christian initiation, and the faithful by calling to mind their baptism, and by acts of penitence' (*Calendarium Romanum, Notae*, 27).

The reference to 'the catechumens' may ring strangely in our ears, which only goes to show how far we have lost any real grasp of the meaning of Lent. Lent originates in the weeks during which the catechumens, to be baptized at the Easter Vigil, underwent their final preparation, which included a number of liturgical functions which the calendar here calls 'the various stages of Christian initiation'. It gradually became the custom for the faithful to associate themselves with the praying and fasting required of the catechumens. Once the catechumenate fell into abeyance, with the nominal total Christianization of Europe, and the consequent lack of adult baptisms, Lent remained as a period of penitential preparation for Easter, but deprived of the baptismal context which alone really gave it meaning, although traces of it survived in the liturgical books.

In a different pastoral situation the catechumenate and its rites have been restored, and will become more and more of a reality in the years to come. And we are all called upon to observe Lent in this baptismal context, 'by calling to mind our baptism', and by repenting of the ways in which we have failed to live up to its implications in our lives, the implications of that paschal mystery which we are to celebrate once more at Easter.

On Sundays 3, 4 and 5 the readings of Year A, which are more overtly baptismal than those of years B and C, may replace the latter, and the proper prefaces reflecting their themes may also be used.

Ash Wednesday

Even Easter people live Lent: your Father who sees all that is done in secret will reward you.

First Reading   Joel 2: 12–18

The call from God to 'come back . . . turn' was a constant call made through his special servants, the prophets. That call was always 'now . . . now'; always with the sense of urgency expressed wonderfully in this reading by appealing to the whole span of society to 'order a fast . . . summon . . . assemble . . . gather . . . lament'. This was prophetic guidance where a severe locust-plague threatened to undermine the hard-won reunion of the nation around the Temple and the Law, once the people had returned from the exile in Babylon (587–539). The purpose was pressing: to win from God 'blessing . . . pity on his people' and redress of the ills which afflicted them. Joel is intent on indicating the need for full interior relinquishment of evil if God is to hear their prayer, to uphold his own honour and, 'jealous on behalf of his land', to dispel the appearance of abandoning his promises.

Responsorial Psalm   51 (50)

℟ *Have mercy on us, O Lord, for we have sinned.*

1 Have mercy on me, God, in your kindness.
   In your compassion blot out my offence.
   O wash me more and more from my guilt
   and cleanse me from my sin. (R)

2 My offences truly I know them;
   my sin is always before me.
   Against you, you alone, have I sinned:
   what is evil in your sight I have done. (R)

3 A pure heart create for me, O God,
   put a steadfast spirit within me.
   Do not cast me away from your presence,
   nor deprive me of your holy spirit. (R)

4 Give me again the joy of your help;
  with a spirit of fervour sustain me,
  O Lord, open my lips
  and my mouth shall declare your praise. (R)

A penitential lament and plea for mercy, this Psalm acknowledges both the need for and the source of purification; that a pure heart can only be won through God's 'kindness . . . compassion . . . presence', and 'the joy of your help'.

Second Reading   2 Corinthians 5: 20–6: 2

Speaking in a time already blessed by the fruits of the resurrection, living the life that fulfils the promise of God in the Old Testament, Paul yet continues the prophetic call to 'be reconciled to God'. For the Christians at Corinth the need was 'not to neglect the grace of God that you *have* received'. The 'now' of this call is all the days between the gift of life by faith in the resurrected Christ, and the full flowering of that life in the experience of Christian perfection. The goal of all effort is to 'become the goodness of God' here on earth. This is the salvation to which God summons his people, and has made possible through Christ.

Gospel   Matthew 6: 1–6, 16–18

Matthew's Gospel is concerned to present the Christian life in its continuance of and divergence from the Old Testament tradition. Jesus' instruction on almsgiving, prayer and fasting shows them capable of winning God's reward only if performed from the proper interior desire. Those who parade these practices, display their true desire, 'to win men's admiration'. In achieving this reward, their hypocrisy has deprived them of the reward from 'the Father in heaven'. Secrecy signifies the simple desire for God's reward, as does happiness in hope. Washing and anointing were Jewish preparations for festivities and banquets, often seen as images of complete, heavenly life. Jesus associates them with the Christian asceticism which, leaving the past in ashes at hearing the Good News, is a training of the grateful heart's thirst for more of the life of God. There is strong assurance of God's will to reward abundantly this thirst of sincere desire.

First Sunday in Lent

The Lenten liturgy conducts the Christian through a scriptural symphony. Old Testament Readings develop the theme of the first movement: God's covenants within history, progressively promising fuller life. The second movement is composed of New Testament readings: exhortation in the exercises of the life of grace lived now. The third movement, Gospel readings, harmonizes the themes of life promised and life lived with proclamations of significant episodes in the Messiah's progress, making possible the fulfilment in the Paschal finale.

First Reading   **Genesis 9: 8–15**

Covenants are compassionate contracts between God and those dependent upon his creative power. The first covenant, with Noah after the flood, is a promise to 'every living creature . . . for all generations'. It is an unconditional declaration from God, on his own initiative of loving goodwill, bringing with it a sign of his eternal fidelity. In ancient times, pagans often viewed the rainbow as a sign of divine disfavour and punishment. The author of this covenant account has inverted such interpretations; the sign of fear and punishment to pagans is source of hope to God's people, because he 'will recall the covenant' that promises continuance of life.

Responsorial Psalm   25 (24)

℟ *Your ways, Lord, are faithfulness and love*
  for those who keep your covenant.

1 Lord, make me know your ways.
  Lord, teach me your paths.
  Make me walk in your truth, and teach me:
  for you are God my saviour. (R)

2 Remember your mercy, Lord,
  and the love you have shown from old.
  In your love remember me,
  because of your goodness, O Lord. (R)

3 The Lord is good and upright.
He shows the path to those who stray,
He guides the humble in the right path;
He teaches his way to the poor. (R)

In an individual prayer for guidance in 'the right path', the psalmist acknowledges God's past mercy and love, and appeals for continued fidelity to the covenant.

Second Reading   **1 Peter 3: 18–22**

This epistle of Peter is often regarded as the first encyclical. It urges Christians to endure all trials and persecutions rather than betray their baptism. Encouragement is rooted in the reason for hope. Jesus Christ has made all things subject to his power, even death, and nothing can oppose his wish 'to lead us to God' – except refusal to believe. In Noah's day, their faith and the ark saved eight people in the purification 'by water', while all who 'refused to believe' perished. Those in the new ark, the Church, are the 'you' addressed by Peter: all who believe and are baptized in the purifying death and resurrection of Christ.

Gospel   **Mark 1: 12–15**

In this passage, Mark presents the final preparation and full proclamation of God's greatest covenant, called in the New Testament 'the kingdom' (of God or of heaven). For Mark's readers, 'the wilderness' and 'the wild beasts' expressed everything in conflict with the ways of God, especially the wiles of Satan, chief evil spirit. Jesus the man, neither beast nor angel, is shown in a symbol of his whole life – holy humanity in mortal combat with temptation to disobey the Spirit who urges and aids him. Jesus emerges from his personal Lent with the victory of the 'Good News from God'. His proclamation is a condensed summary of his whole prophetic teaching. After centuries of hope and preparation 'the time has come' for men to receive the fullness of the covenant promises: 'the kingdom of God'. This means the decisive defeat of everything opposed to God, his ruling authority over all; the wilderness victory is extended to the whole world. The kingdom can be entered only through one gate, obedience to the command 'Repent, and believe the Good News'.

Second Sunday in Lent

Who can be against us? God will not refuse anything to his Beloved.

First Reading   **Genesis 22: 1–2, 9–13, 15–18**

This most celebrated story of the patriarchal era shows the development of Israel beyond the human sacrifices common to other religions of the day. The intention of the passage is to demonstrate the way in which the one God, 'the Lord', conducts his freely chosen relations with Israel. The Lord deals personally with Abraham. His love is shown in promises. These promises need the faith of Abraham to be performed. Faith had already won a promised son, despite Abraham's and Sarah's old age (Genesis 18: 10). With the promise of further descendants, 'Isaac the reward of faith becomes the test of that same faith'. Abraham's tested trust in God's power to fulfil his promise, even when the usual procedures seem to make it impossible, brings from God the most solemn convenantal declaration – 'I swear by my own self' – in a promise of even greater gifts as reward of obedience. The whole experience takes place on the mountain – the privileged place of sacrifice to God, and of receiving his revelation.

Responsorial Psalm   **116 (115)**

℟ *I will walk in the presence of the Lord*
  in the land of the living.

1 I trusted, even when I said:
  'I am sorely afflicted'.
  O precious in the eyes of the Lord
  is the death of his faithful. (R)

2 Your servant, Lord, your servant am I;
  you have loosened my bonds.
  A thanksgiving sacrifice I make:
  I will call on the Lord's name. (R)

3 My vows to the Lord I will fulfil
  before all his people,
  in the courts of the house of the Lord,
  in your midst, O Jerusalem. (R)

A thanksgiving Psalm upon deliverance from death and enemies, this passage expresses renewed obedience to God who holds the psalmist too precious to be abandoned to death.

Second Reading   **Romans 8: 31–34**

This reading is part of Paul's appeal to Roman Christians to remember the history of God's generosity as certain proof of his continual wish and power 'to benefit us all'. God's refusal of nothing in performing his promised acts of love recalls Abraham's imitation of this fidelity to the covenant. Yet God gives even more; what was allowed Abraham, God did not allow himself: 'God did not spare his own Son, but gave him up'. This is definite demonstration that God is 'on our side . . . has chosen (us) and acquits' us of the sentence of death. Christ Jesus imitated his Father's generosity while on earth, and continues to do so by having risen, standing before and pleading with God for us.

Gospel   **Mark 9: 2–10**

The transfiguration tells of the new era initiated by the latest of God's servants, because of his identity as Son. The tale is set on a mountain – scene of Abraham's test, of Moses' meeting with God, of the reception of the Law (Exodus 34) and of many important divine revelations. Mark's story presents these earlier episodes as preparatory anticipation of the supreme event of revelation in Jesus. Moses and Elijah stand for the whole Old Testament period, recorded in the Scriptures, which the rabbis divided into two traditions, the Law and the Prophets. This presence with Jesus is evidence of their companionship in the progressive plan of God to give life to his people. The cloud is the *shekinah*, the sign of God's *presence* with his elect (Exodus 24: 15). The supreme stature of Jesus is shown once the voice has spoken – he stands alone, above even Moses and Elijah in honour. The voice declares this honour is due to his Sonship. The 'Son' recalls the hope in Daniel (ch. 7) of a Son of Man to bring in the new age, and Isaiah's belief that it would be brought through the obedient suffering of the 'servant' (Isaiah 42: 1).

Third Sunday in Lent

Take all this out of here and stop turning my Father's house into a market.

First Reading   Exodus 20: 1–17

This passage is part of Israel's account of her birth as a nation. Delivered from slavery, guided towards a new land and life, the Sinai experience is the story of a people's inspiration to protect and preserve its identity as the elect of God. The ten commandments were the root of the wisdom that flowered in the Law. The Law outlined the obligations of obedience to the covenant as an aid to living interior loving gratitude. All aids are easily abused, and external obligations were often to be used as avoidance of interior obedience in Israel's future. Even the ethical excellence of Israel's Law was no substitute for 'the heart held wholly open'.

Responsorial Psalm   19 (18)

℞ *You, Lord, have the message of eternal life.*

1 The law of the Lord is perfect,
   it revives the soul.
   The rule of the Lord is to be trusted,
   it gives wisdom to the simple. (R)

2 The precepts of the Lord are right,
   They gladden the heart.
   The command of the Lord is clear,
   it gives light to the eyes. (R)

3 The fear of the Lord is holy,
   abiding forever,
   The decrees of the Lord are truth
   and all of them just. (R)

4 They are more to be desired than gold,
   than the purest of gold
   and sweeter are they than honey,
   than honey from the comb. (R)

A hymn of praise, celebrating God's glory and his guidance through the Law. The Law's description as 'perfect . . . to be trusted . . . right' is derived from its effects: it 'revives the soul . . . gives wisdom . . . gladdens the heart'. The 'fear of the Lord' is that holy obedience which discerns the way to God's truth.

Second Reading   **1 Corinthians 1: 22–25**

Paul reminds the Christians that it is response to his preaching which has won them their new life – and he preached 'a crucified Christ'. There is to be no compromise on this difficult paradox, the mystery that can be accepted by only 'those who have been called'. The 'Jews' and 'Greeks' represent those attitudes which close the heart to God's call to faith: willing to believe only when expectations of divine magnificence are satisfied, or when what is preached conforms to previous philosophical outlooks. A crucified Christ as 'the power and wisdom of God' (terms often earlier applied to the Law) can be accepted once one has risen to the perspective of God himself, 'wiser than human wisdom', and yielded to a power 'stronger than human strength'.

Gospel   **John 2: 13–25**

The Passover was the Jewish celebration of God's deliverance of Israel from slavery, the beginning of the birth of the nation as the People of God. The Law contained many obligations of worship in the Temple, sign and seal of the covenant. Many saw such acts as satisfying conditions for God's continued favour. Passover involved the sacrifice of animals, conveniently sold on site. Since only special coinage could be used in the Temple, other merchants sold these to the people. In John's account, Jesus' anger at the arrangement goes beyond a purification of corruptions. The old will be replaced by a new temple: the resurrected body of Christ, the Church, entered by faith. 'Take all this out of here' can be seen to refer to attitudes which perpetuate the illusion of a system of exchange which reduces obedience to the Father to 'a market'. Only one exchange is valid: belief because of the great sign of Jesus' resurrection. Belief in other signs is at best instructive, and not to be trusted fully.

Fourth Sunday in Lent

'God sent his Son into the world not to condemn the world, but so that through him the world might be saved.'

First Reading   **2 Chronicles 36: 14–16, 19–23**

'There was no further remedy': this is the verdict of the Chronicler on the exile in Babylon. God's wish 'to spare his people' had shown itself through the guidance of the Law, the prophets and the Temple consecration, but infidelity to the covenant and imitation of pagan 'shameful practices' meant severe measures of purification. The exile is viewed through the eyes of Jeremiah – a return to the days of the Sinai wilderness when Israel could be proud of only her God, and learn to rest in him alone. The author is at pains to present the covenant with David as even superior to that with Moses. The promised continuity of kingly wisdom, bringing a prosperous security and pure piety found expression in the Temple in Jerusalem. Destroyed by enemies, who unwittingly carried out the sentence of God, the Temple and Israel's glory are to be restored to her after her purification. Such promises were to be proved feeble until the full presence of God was revealed in Jesus.

Responsorial Psalm   **137 (136)**

℟ *O let my tongue*
   cleave my mouth
   if I remember you not!

1 By the rivers of Babylon
  there we sat and wept,
  remembering Zion;
  on the poplars that grew there
  we hung up our harps. (R)

2 For it was there that they asked us,
  our captors, for songs,
  our oppressors, for joy.
  'Sing to us,' they said,
  'one of Zion's songs.' (R)

3 O how could we sing
  the song of the Lord
  on alien soil?
  If I forget you, Jerusalem,
  let my right hand wither! (R)

4 O let my tongue
  cleave to my mouth
  if I remember you not,
  if I prize not Jerusalem
  above all my joys! (R)

This famous Psalm of community lament expresses the desperate sense of loss during the exile. Deprived of consolation, the psalmist can see no path to peace and piety except by a return to what has been lost: the land, the worship and the Jerusalem temple.

Second Reading   **Ephesians 2: 4–10**

From the beginning God has meant us to live the good life, and in Christ Jesus he has achieved his aim. Such is the resounding message of this epistle, an exhortation to a community already developing beyond earlier expectations of Jesus' immediate return. The Christian has been 'brought to life with Christ' and lives a life of unity with the whole body of Christ (4: 1–16) having received 'a place with him in heaven'. The offer and acceptance of the gifts of God are derived from the love which wishes 'to show for all ages to come . . . how infinitely rich he is in grace'. The metaphor of his people as 'God's work of art' beautifully recalls the prophetic vision of God moulding his people like a potter his clay.

Gospel   **John 3: 14–21**

This passage is part of a long discourse in John's Gospel on the New Birth that Christ has made possible. The episode of the serpent is that recounted in Numbers 21: 4–9, the healing of sickness unto death. The serpent is a symbol of salvation (Wisdom 16: 6f.) and Jesus employs it as a help to explaining his mission and the means of salvation that he offers. Mere sight of the serpent lifted up brought healing; belief in the Son lifted up brings eternal life. The word for 'lifted up' refers both to the raising upon the cross and raising from the dead. Those who did not see the serpent died, as those who do not believe in the Son condemn themselves to darkness, since failure to believe is considered refusal, as preference for darkness and fear of exposing personal evil to purifying light.

Fifth Sunday in Lent

'When I am lifted up from the earth I shall draw all men to myself.'

First Reading   **Jeremiah 31: 31–34**

All the covenants and compassionate creativity of God in the history of Israel had one aim, the perfect accomplishment of the divine desire: 'I will be their God and they shall be my people'. Brought to humiliation and exile, Israel after centuries had not been able to satisfy this wish. It is to Jeremiah that we owe the bold insight of the reason for Israel's radical incapacity. The covenant communicated the path to perfection, but could not provide the power to perform the necessary obedience. Writing the law on hearts, deep within, as contrasted with writing on tablets of stone (Exodus 31: 18) or in a book (Exodus 24: 7) – this metaphor is Jeremiah's vision of what the Lord will accomplish among those who receive the new covenant. Equipped with an immediate knowledge of God and his eternal forgiveness of sin, all will be teachers of God's truth – as expected in the Messianic era (Isaiah 54: 13).

Responsorial Psalm   51 (50)

℟ *A pure heart create for me, O God.*

1 Have mercy on me, God, in your kindness,
   In your compassion blot out my offence.

O wash me more and more from my guilt
and cleanse me from my sin. (R)

2 A pure heart create for me, O God,
put a steadfast spirit within me.
Do not cast me away from your presence,
nor deprive me of your holy spirit. (R)

3 Give me again the joy of your help;
with a spirit of fervour sustain me,
that I may teach transgressors your ways
and sinners may return to you. (R)

Pleading for purification from guilt and sin, the psalmist seeks to
share that holy spirit of steadfast fervour which tutors the teachers of
God's ways.

Second Reading   **Hebrews 5: 7–9**

The epistle to the Hebrews exults in the humanity of Jesus, the
vehicle of his perfection as compassionate high priest of the people.
While not denying the pre-existence of Christ as the Word with God,
the author concentrates on the earthly process that brought Jesus to
perfect the presence of the Word in his personality. This was
achieved through obedience to the Word within him, an obedience
aided not harmed by his suffering human burdens and oppositions.
It was to God, not just to suffering, that Jesus submitted – in itself a
pure and humble prayer to the power who alone can save. Once and
for all Christ has broken through the power of evil which prevents
obedience to the Word.

Gospel   **John 12: 20–33**

Before Jesus endures the new Passover on the cross, calling it 'the
hour . . . for the Son of Man to be glorified', John presents his
endeavours to educate the disciples in its meaning. He employs
two examples from ordinary life. The function of grain is fertility,
and a single seed achieves harvest by death. All who cling to what
they have, close themselves to further fruition in life. Jesus acknowledges that natural dread of the hour of death, a reminder of the
agony in Gethsemane, but moves beyond all appearances to the

reality – God will glorify himself and his Son because of it. A voice from heaven aids the attempt to educate the disciples, another example of Jesus' conviction that his Father was also bearing witness in his life to the truth of his word. As often, the disciples misinterpret matters – a fact to be remedied fully only by faith after the resurrection. Instruction is urgent not only to prepare for Jesus' Paschal mystery, but for the disciples' own participation as followers and servants of Christ. By 'the kind of death he would die' Jesus will be able to assist them to persevere; the power of the resurrected Christ will draw them and will not fail to provide fidelity.

HOLY WEEK

Liturgical Introduction

Holy Week, and more particularly the *Paschal Triduum* (which begins with the evening Eucharist of the Lord's Supper on Maundy Thursday and ends with Vespers on Easter Day), is the climax of the liturgical year, to which everything else leads, or from which it derives.

Outwardly we celebrate a succession of events: the entry into Jerusalem on Palm Sunday; the last supper on Maundy Thursday; the sufferings and death of the Lord on Good Friday; his rising in victory on Easter Day. Such an observance is very old, originating in Jerusalem in the fourth century; but it is not primitive – the primitive observance is of the Lord's *Pasch*, his Passover ('pass-over') on Easter night, recalling the whole redemptive mystery of passion and resurrection in one liturgical action. And we need to understand the celebrations of Holy Week as forming an integral whole. It is the celebration of the passover of the Lord from death to life; and it is also the celebration of *our* passover from death to life 'through him and with him and in him'. In the services of Holy Week we participate – 'in mystery', sacramentally – in the events they re-call and re-present, in the acts whereby the Christ redeemed the world: 'dying he destroyed our death; rising he restored our life'. And we thereby look forward to that final passover from death to life, when he will come in glory.

And it is of the essence of this paschal liturgy that the Easter Vigil combines the theme of the Lord's resurrection with the theme of baptism, for it is by baptism that the Christian is first grafted into Christ, is made partaker of his death and resurrection, is made partaker of his passover. And even when the Easter Vigil has to be celebrated without the baptism, confirmation and first communion of the new members of Christ which should form the central part of it, our own baptism is recalled in the renewal of our baptismal promises, leading to our Easter communion. We renew our· commitment to sharing the passover of the Lord, and he renews in us the sharing of his risen life.

59

Passion (Palm) Sunday

Hosanna! Blessings on him who comes in the name of the Lord!

Gospel of the Procession   **Mark 11: 1–10**

Jerusalem was the centre and symbol of Judaism, the city of God. Hopes for the establishment of God's kingdom among his people naturally focused on Jerusalem as the scene for the Messiah's success. Mark's Gospel describes Jesus' entry into Jerusalem in terms of those hopes – but carefully controls the concept of success. Knowing the outcome of his entry to their city, Jesus nevertheless permits the people their time of celebration with a poignancy shared by Christians who read the incident knowing that the joy will turn to rejection. As he will in preparing for the Passover meal (14: 13–16), Jesus employs a foresight of circumstances and people's reactions to modify expectations of his mission. Greeted as God's Messiah, 'in the name of the Lord', he comes on a colt. Heralded as initiating the promised Davidic prosperity, his kingdom will come through humility and lowliness. Nevertheless success is assured; celebration is appropriate.

First Reading   **Isaiah 50: 4–7**

This is the third of the songs which refer to a suffering servant. The figure of the servant made a massive contribution to Israel's development beyond a simple association of suffering and sin. Secure in his knowledge of God's word, wishing to use God's gift for the weary, his suffering becomes a paradoxical sign of his innocence. The insults and opposition he meets, demonstrate not punishment of a sinner, but the ignorance of those who abuse him, and their deafness to God's prophets. Even so, his fidelity to the word of God will not be defeated: he will endure all and 'not be shamed'.

Responsorial Psalm   22 (21)

℞ *My God, my God, why have you forsaken me?*
1 All who see me deride me.
  They curl their lips, they toss their heads.

'He trusted in the Lord, let him save him;
let him release him if this is his friend'. (R)

2 Many dogs have surrounded me,
a band of the wicked beset me.
They tear holes in my hands and my feet
I can count every one of my bones. (R)

3 They divide my clothing among them.
They cast lots for my robe.
O Lord, do not leave me alone,
my strength, make haste to help me! (R)

4 I will tell your name to my brethren
and praise you where they are assembled.
'You who fear the Lord give him praise;
all sons of Jacob, give him glory.
Revere him, Israel's sons.' (R)

A poetic lament in the midst of dreadful distress, this Psalm progresses through an account of suffering to a communal thanksgiving for deliverance. The first quotation reflects the belief that suffering indicates sinfulness, innocent men being God's friends and protected from pain.

Second Reading   **Philippians 2: 6–11**

A liturgical hymn, containing an early confession of the core of Christian belief, this text was used by Paul in his exhortations to the Philippians to live as Christ lived, in humility before God. The poetic structure swings like a pendulum, from the heights of Christ's pre-existent divinity, down into 'death on a cross', then up to his exalted state as Lord, 'the name . . . above all other names'. Christ is the subject in the downward deeds; it is God in his grace who performs the acts leading upward to exaltation.

Passion   **Mark 14: 1–15: 47**

Mark's passion narrative presents the crowning completion of the Messiah's work. Crucial to interpreting the events as anything other than the lonely death of a condemned man is the identity of 'the criminal'. Writing with hindsight, having known the identity in the

61

resurrection experience, the evangelist includes more than mere history. He creates a theological account which witnesses to the truth of that history. Jesus was innocent: his condemnation is shown as the wish of Pilate to placate the crowd, a feeble outcome of false and conflicting evidence. Jesus was abandoned. Betrayed by one of the beloved twelve, deserted by all in the garden (dramatically emphasized by the young man's naked escape), disowned by Peter and discredited by even companions in crucifixion, Jesus repeats the psalmist's typically human cry, 'Why?' (Psalm 22: 1). Only the belief that Scripture shows all this to be in accord with God's plan of deliverance sustains the explanation of events as messianic. Schooled in the Scriptures, Jesus the prophet accepts his fate as fruitful. To the apostles, he extends the cup of submission to bitter death but transformed into the eucharist, the blood which brings them the sweetness of life in the new covenant. He faithfully endures what he has foreseen, silent before stubborn refusal to see him as he is. Even so, the mystery moves towards revelation. Often evaded or avoided by Jesus in the course of this whole Gospel, the issue of his identity surfaces above the shrouds of secrecy. With necessary qualification from Son-of-Man Scriptures, he acknowledges his identity as 'the Christ'. Killed and crowned, with malicious irony, as king, he is revealed, with merciful equal irony, to the gentile centurion as Son of God. For his followers death seemed to be defeat. There remained only 'some women . . . watching from a distance'.

Holy Thursday

He showed how perfect his love was: 'Do this as a memorial of me'.

First Reading   **Exodus 12: 1–8, 11–14**

The feast later known as Passover dates from before the Egyptian slavery. A sacrifice of animals was made to ensure the fertility of flocks at spring time. Blood and death were always mysterious allies of life. The ancient feast was infinitely enhanced by association with the exodus. At the summit of God's deeds of deliverance, the meal 'in honour of the Lord' and the blood from the sacrificial victim mark the life of the Israelites as God's elect. It is the death of their enemies which delivers them to freedom, to the fertility of life as God's beloved. The Lord commands continual remembrance of this day of deliverance, and celebration in honour of his gifts of life. Later reflections on sabbath ceremonies saw in them a reliving of the exodus and election, and a renewal of its effects.

Responsorial Psalm   **116 (115)**

℞ *The blessing-cup that we bless*
  is a communion with the blood of Christ.

1 How can I repay the Lord
   for his goodness to me?
   The cup of salvation I will raise;
   I will call on the Lord's name. (R)

2 O precious in the eyes of the Lord
   is the death of his faithful.
   Your servant, Lord, your servant am I;
   you have loosened my bonds. (R)

3 A thanksgiving sacrifice I make;
   I will call on the Lord's name.
   My vows to the Lord I will fulfil
   before all his people. (R)

The psalmist recites his hymn of thanksgiving for deliverance while making an offering in the Temple. 'The cup of salvation' is a symbol for God's creative generosity, and in the thought of the day contrasted with 'the cup of his wrath'.

Second Reading   **1 Corinthians 11: 23–26**

The earliest known record of the Christian eucharist. It presents the celebration as memorial and preparation. The community of the Church, enlivened by the Spirit of her risen Lord – 'the new covenant in my blood' – makes present by memorial the liberating sacrifice which created her. Strengthened by the anticipation of that final perfection of her life in God, when 'the Lord comes', the Church proclaims the Lord's death as the foundation of her reasons for hope. It was the death of her friend which delivered her into freedom, the life of grace. Strongest of the parallels with Old Testament covenants sealed in blood is that of Sinai (Exodus 24: 8). Eating and drinking are emphasized as acts of full participation in the memorial, as baptism involves the Christian's full participation in the death and resurrection of him whose memorial is celebrated (cf. 1 Corinthians 10: 16f.).

Gospel   **John 13: 1–15**

With the scene at the last supper John begins the second half of his Gospel, the Book of Exaltation. It is another of the great 'signs', accompanied by teaching, by which the disciples are invited into and instructed in the life of faith. John's account of this evening differs from the synoptics' by having no explicit institution of the eucharist. Its absence here, however, serves to highlight the theology of the Bread of Life (ch. 6) which, with the teaching on divine life in this chapter, underlies all the sacramental life of the Church. That divine life is shown to be lived on earth as a humble service of the brethren. Knowing that the hour of his death was close, that 'the Father had put everything into his hands', Jesus chose the duties of a Jewish house-servant as his last parable-in-action before the crucifixion. The whole of the Christian's life is to be a loving service in memory of the Master. Washing would have inevitably recalled to John's readers the baptism which initiated them into the divine life of the Church, the fruit of faith. Peter's objections reflect a misunderstanding but not the lack of desire to have all 'in common with' Christ. The betrayal of Judas, on the other hand, reflects the sad possibility of refusal to yield interiorly to grace, even when water has signified its gift.

Good Friday

By his sufferings shall God's servant justify many: by his wounds we are healed.

First Reading   **Isaiah 52: 13–53: 12**

This, the fourth song of the suffering servant, comes closer than all other Old Testament theology to Christian truth. The Jewish teachers, in the time of Jesus, did not interpret this passage as pointing to God's Messiah (i.e. chosen servant), but Jesus saw it as indicating the mystery of how God's promise of salvation was to be achieved. It was of enormous help to early Christian explanation of the death of Christ. Perhaps the most powerful of all Old Testament poets, the author achieves a dramatic sense of incongruity in his scenes. Lovingly presented by God as 'my servant . . . exalted . . . praying for sinners' the man is perceived by his fellows as 'a thing despised and rejected . . . struck by God' for his personal sins. Real as his oppression was, no less real, with hindsight, was his mysterious expiation of evil. 'Harshly dealt with . . . though he had done no wrong' his pain substituted for the punishment of sinners, his goodness atoned for their evil, and 'through him what the Lord wishes will be done'. The whole is an image of the ideal son of God, but unrealized at the time of writing.

Responsorial Psalm   31 (30)

℞ *Father, into your hands I commend my spirit.*

1 In you, O Lord, I take refuge.
   Let me never be put to shame.
   In your justice, set me free.
   Into your hands I commend my spirit.
   It is you who will redeem me, Lord. (R)

2 In the face of all my foes
   I am a reproach,
   an object of scorn to my neighbours
   and of fear to my friends. (R)

3 Those who see me in the street
run far away from me.
I am like a dead man, forgotten in men's hearts,
like a thing thrown away. (R)

4 But as for me, I trust in you, Lord,
I say: 'You are my God'.
My life is in your hands, deliver me
from the hands of those who hate me. (R)

5 Let your face shine on your servant.
Save me in your love.
Be strong, let your heart take courage,
all who hope in the Lord. (R)

An individual laments extreme distress and abandonment 'like a dead man'. Nevertheless he prays to God for deliverance, trusting in the power above all pain: 'My life is in your hands'.

Second Reading   **Hebrews 4: 14–16; 5: 7–9**

The high priest was the mediator, the one through whom God's mercy came to the community. He alone entered the inner sanctuary of the Temple to receive from God the favour to be bestowed on the faithful. This epistle speaks of the exalted Jesus as 'the supreme high priest'. Being Son of God he is infinitely more able to mediate mercy. His sanctuary being the very 'highest heaven' he is infinitely more endowed with God's grace. At the same time his personal involvement with human needs assures the community of sympathetic compassion for their weaknesses. Jesus' ministry of mediation began 'during his life on earth': his perfection as priest was won in the school of suffering and the power of his prayer ordained him as 'the source of eternal salvation'. The professed faith in the earthly ministry will provide confidence in its heavenly continuation.

Passion   **John 18: 1–19: 42**

John's extraordinary account of the Passion dramatically extends the insights of resurrection-faith which control the synoptic tradition. He offers the testimony 'of one who saw it . . . that you may believe as well'. He saw in the Passion the history of a victory, and boldly

66

portrays the crucifixion as an act of glorification, screened by sheer event but seen truly from within the resurrection experience. This emphasis is served by the literary restraint in the scenes of oppression: there is no agony in Gethsemane, the mockery is minimized and made to serve the irony surrounding Jesus' kingship. The crucifixion becomes a deed of Jesus, not something done to him. It is the great sign of shrouded glory. 'Knowing everything that was going to happen to him', Jesus still steps forward, taking the initiative from the start. On the arrival of 'the traitor' and in reaction to Peter's impetuous aggression, he appears almost eager to embrace his cruel end! In contrast to the silence in the synoptic accounts, he speaks out so boldly that the guard slaps him. In extreme antithesis to Peter's fearful denial of himself as a disciple – 'I am not' – Jesus openly acknowledges his identity – 'I am he', 'I am a king'. It is not only the evangelist who knows all is in fulfilment of Scripture, but Jesus who exhibits such knowledge. Events even fulfil his own words. In the discourse with Pilate, Jesus is shown stage-centre, continuing his work of summoning men to faith in the truth. The cross looms large among those signs which demand a choice: rather than a 'kingdom not of this world', Pilate and the crowd choose Caesar, king of 'the world' in opposition to God. Stretched on the cross Jesus still continues his service of those he loves. He creates a new relationship between his mother and his believing beloved, born of his death. In command even at the point of death, he completes his obedient fulfilment of Scripture, and rests in the accomplishment of the great work of glorification.

Easter Vigil

God saw all he had made, and indeed it was very good: 'He is going before you . . . you will see him.'

Old Testament Readings

Genesis 1: 1–2: 2

Psalm 104 (103): 1–2, 5–6, 10, 12–14, 24, 35
or 33 (32): 4–7, 12–13, 20, 22

	Genesis 22: 1–18
Psalm	16 (15): 5, 8–11
	Exodus 14: 15–15: 1
Psalm	Exodus 15: 1–7a, 17–18
	Isaiah 54: 5–14
Psalm	30 (29): 1–5, 10–12
	Isaiah 55: 1–11
Psalm	Isaiah 12: 2–6
	Baruch 3: 9–15, 32–4: 4
Psalm	19 (18): 7–10
	Ezekiel 36: 16–17a, 18–28
Psalm	42 (41): 1–2, 4; 43 (42): 3–4
or	51 (50): 10–13, 16–17

On Easter night all time is telescoped to focus on the pivotal event of human history. The Church in vigil adopts the posture of the pre-Christian world: poised for the satisfaction of a supreme desire, aroused to a hope by God's promise in history, watching for the dawn of God's glory displayed. For those to be baptized it is commemoration of all that has made their new creation possible. For those in the way, it is refreshment also, and renewal of faith in the God who has power to subject all things to their salvation.

It is God's powerful word which begins time (Reading 1). Effortlessly creating all that has life, God is drawn by delight in his own work to crown it with man, his own image and likeness. All things are given for his fertility in every way. Control of light and water are especially divine powers, and the Psalm tells of them as shackled to man's needs. The second reading shows God as teacher, providing that schooling in faith without which sin's slavery cannot be pierced by the flow of God's goodness. Terrible though the trials may be, Abraham and his heirs of faith will triumph in God's power above all powers, if, as the Psalm proclaims, their desire for him is above all desires.

Exodus is an exuberant celebration of the creator God using all creation in a strategy for salvation. Present among his people, he commands even the co-operation of 'light . . . wind . . . water', like

a divine general marshalling his obedient troops. The greatness of
God is shown by his works: such is the song of Moses, some of the
oldest poetry in the Bible.

Isaiah accounts for the history of God's people: it is the fruit of the
compelling love of her divine husband. Not even difficult periods of
division, neither the flood nor exile, can quench his compassionate
ardour to consummate a covenant of peace with his beloved. They
are but as tears in the night, 'but joy comes with dawn'.

The prophet persists in the hope for eventual satisfaction (Reading 5), when in a joyful banquet of messianic marriage, God's gifts
will quench all thirsts and feed all hungers. As water provides all
fertility, so will God's word ensure this satisfaction, since it flows
from a fathomless well of saving power.

Baruch believes desire for godly light has already a guide, the Law
which extends the wisdom of God himself to his 'well-beloved'.
Seasons and stars 'gladly shine for their creator'. This will be Israel's
glory, 'more to be desired than gold'.

The revelation to Ezekiel summarizes all this history. All has been
because of God's desire: 'You shall be my people and I will be your
God'. Distracted from this as her deepest wish, Israel can claim no
right to redress; but her return to a home with God will be accomplished by definite demonstration of her Lord's holiness and merciful
love, a washing away of past sin and participation in his own spirit.
The final psalm describes the faithful remnant as though on Easter
night: 'thirsting for God' yet impotent to do aught but wait. This
night will answer all hope, and the question 'when can I enter and see
the face of God?'

New Testament Reading **Romans 6: 3–11**

Paul resoundingly proclaims the reality of the new creation. Christ
Jesus is the first to have realized the desire of the ages – an obedient
passage through life, death and burial, and beyond into the resurrected 'life with God'. God's glory, through Christ, has defeated
death and sin, and satisfied the divine desire to share his own life
with creation. Achieved by one, it is possible for all. By baptism
Christians have undergone, 'with Christ', a death to their 'former

69

selves'. They live a new life 'in Christ'. Their faith assures them of future perfection, a full participation in Christ's resurrection.

Responsorial Psalm   118 (117)

℟ *Alleluia, alleluia, alleluia!*

1 Alleluia!
Give thanks to the Lord for he is good,
for his love has no end.
Let the sons of Israel say:
'His love has no end'. (R)

2 The Lord's right hand has triumphed;
his right hand has raised me up.
I shall not die, I shall live
and recount his deeds. (R)

3 The stone which the builders rejected
has become the corner stone.
This is the work of the Lord,
a marvel in our eyes. (R)

This Psalm of thanksgiving was aptly interpreted by early Christians as referring to Christ (Acts 4: 11). All is accomplished in God's marvellous work of love.

Gospel   **Mark 16: 1–8**

Nobody witnessed the moment of resurrection; nobody could. If the women to whom it was first revealed knew fear, it was the fear accompanying all divine disclosures. Mark describes the finding of the empty tomb with the emphasis on a new beginning. 'Very early . . . first day . . . as the sun was rising' are often associated with the light which the resurrection has shone on the world. Coming to treat a corpse, the women are taught that Jesus has finished with death: 'he has risen, he is not here'. As they have seen, so are they commanded to go and tell – as will the Church until all see him.

EASTER

Easter Day

This is the work of the Lord, a marvel in our eyes: 'he saw and believed'.

First Reading   **Acts 10: 34, 37–43**

Peter preaches from experience, and summons all to share in the forgiveness of sin through belief in Jesus. The content of his message is the *kerygma*, the core of Christian preaching. He describes the history that has led to his preaching – the good works of Jesus in the power of the Holy Spirit, the killing of him by those he sought to cure, then God's activity in raising him and allowing him to be seen. Peter, and those with him, are witnesses to it all and, privileged beyond all others in the experience of the resurrected Christ, proclaim the fulfilment of prophetic hope: 'Jesus is Lord'.

Responsorial Psalm   **118 (117)**

℟ *This day was made by the Lord;*
we rejoice and are glad.
or *Alleluia!*

1 Alleluia!
Give thanks to the Lord for he is good,
for his love has no end.
Let the sons of Israel say:
'His love has no end.' (R)

2 The Lord's right hand has triumphed;
his right hand raised me up.
I shall not die, I shall live
and recount his deeds. (R)

3 The stone which the builders rejected
has become the corner stone.
This is the work of the Lord,
a marvel in our eyes. (R)

Easily applicable to the Christian's life, the joy of the psalmist is also infinitely extended by the raising of Jesus. God has established a rejected saviour as source of salvation. The Christian will not die but live the life of God and sing of his glorious love.

Second Reading   **Colossians 3: 1–4**

The epistle to the Colossians expresses Christ's complete victory, 'sitting at God's right hand'. The effect of his resurrection is to introduce the Christian to a 'no-man's land'. Only by the bold assertion 'you have died' can he adequately convey the reality of the Christian's state. His old life is lost to him, his new is 'hidden with Christ in God'. Only at the end of time, 'when Christ is revealed,' will he be fully mature in his true identity, only then will he fully be in possession of life, for Christ has become his life. Meanwhile he may taste his 'true life with Christ' in longing for 'the things that are in heaven'. That thoughts should not be on the things of earth is not a denial of their goodness, but wise counsel to those who now have a thirst for the heavenly. This desire can be satisfied by no earthly thing, and will leave the Christian heart restless until it rests in God.

Alternative Second Reading   **1 Corinthians 5: 6–8**

Paul uses the metaphor of leaven in this passage to express the corruptive influence of evil. It is a reference to the Jewish custom of destroying all leaven in preparation for the paschal feast during which only unleavened bread was allowed. 'Christ our Passover' was already a traditional appellation of Jesus and referred to Christ as our Paschal Lamb, the effective sign of our liberation from the bondage of evil, just as the Jewish rite commemorated the liberation of the Jews from slavery in Egypt by the Exodus. It expressed, therefore, the redemptive aspect of his death. The New Passover is celebrated by 'getting rid of the yeast of evil and wickedness, having only the unleavened bread of sincerity and truth'.

Gospel **John 20: 1–9**

John tells of the empty tomb's discovery in terms of a new dawn. Light and sight are often employed in his Gospel when treating of faith, and this story uses them in a testimony to the first faith in resurrection. Some physical facts differ from the synoptic parallels, but John's version still has much to suggest the use of trustworthy witness. His selection of aspects in the evidence shows his skill in focussing on a truth. That it was 'still dark' may denote not only the time of day, but all time before the resurrected 'light of the world'. Mary can explain what she sees only by usual experience – the removal of a corpse by men. Peter sees more. While he goes 'right into the tomb' and sees the linen cloths, we are yet to be told of 'the other disciple' (probably John). He sees what they saw – but sees beyond. Perhaps because he was known to have surpassed others in love for Jesus; he it is on whom the light of faith shines first: 'He saw and believed'. It is from within this new sight of faith that understanding flows; as promised in scriptural history, 'Jesus is risen'.

Second Sunday of Easter

First Reading **Acts 4: 32–35**

Luke's information about early apostolic history was rather meagre. There were considerable gaps among the individual situations and the teaching elements that made up his material. So, like Mark, he used the 'summary' technique to fill in the gaps and to give the impression of continuous history (see Mark 1: 39; 3: 10–12; Acts 2: 42–47). The generalized sharing of possessions outlined in this present summary (see vv. 32, 34–35) has probably been derived from single occurrences which tradition supplied (see Acts 4: 36–37; 5: 1–4). This universal sharing of goods is a product of later idealizing. Indeed, two distinct ideas emerge from the summary: that things were possessed in common in the first Christian community; and, that there were individuals who sold what they possessed for distribution. The first idea conforms to the contemporary Greek ideal of community life; the second more to the Old Testament ideal as stated in the book of Deuteronomy: 'there shall be no poor amongst us' (Deuteronomy 15: 4). Luke's 'communistic' picture in this passage is not so much a historical account as an ideal for the infant Church – the unity of things spiritual and material.

Responsorial Psalm   118 (117)

℞ *Give thanks to the Lord for he is good,*
  for his love has no end.
  or *Alleluia!*

1 Let the sons of Israel say:
  'His love has no end.'
  Let the sons of Aaron say:
  'His love has no end.'
  Let those who fear the Lord say:
  'His love has no end.' (R)

2 The Lord's right hand has triumphed;
  his right hand raised me up.
  I shall not die, I shall live
  and recount his deeds.
  I was punished, I was punished by the Lord,
  but not doomed to die. (R)

3 The stone which the builders rejected
  has become the corner stone.
  This is the work of the Lord,
  a marvel in our eyes.
  This day was made by the Lord;
  we rejoice and are glad. (R)

This hymn (cf. p. 12) belongs to the Hallel Psalms (see p. 78). The setting is probably a liturgy of thanksgiving. The liberation from which the psalmist has been delivered is applied here to the liberation achieved through Christ's death and resurrection.

Second Reading   1 John 5: 1–6

The connection between two essential elements of Christianity, faith and love, is introduced to the reader. Belief in Jesus makes one a child of God. If we love God we should also love God's children. This love of both Father and children is made manifest by keeping the commandments. The commandments are not difficult because the great hindrance, the world, has already been overcome. Jesus has overcome the world (the symbol of the power of darkness and sin) through his death and resurrection, and any person who 'believes that Jesus is the Son of God' can likewise conquer the world.

Gospel   **John 20: 19–31**

This double episode makes up the Johannine conclusion to the history of the exaltation of Jesus, and its contrast is significant. John's attention is still fixed on Easter Sunday (vv. 19ff.). He simply notes the spiritual qualities of Jesus' risen body without explaining the fact of it. Though Jesus' resurrected body had these spiritual qualities the references to the physical aspects – the wounds in his hands and side – testify to the return of the very Jesus they had known so well. Jesus then confers his mission on the disciples. This mission or commission is to perpetuate the work of divine salvation accomplished in Christ. It is signified by the sacramental act of breathing on them – an effective sign conferring the Spirit, accompanied by the power and authority to express Christ's character. The incident concerning Thomas is included as a fitting end to the story of Jesus – an act of faith, the most explicit expression of faith to be found in the Gospels. The more general conclusion and summing up of the signs that Jesus worked shows that the Gospel has been written for Christian readers, in order to deepen their faith and understanding.

Third Sunday of Easter

First Reading   **Acts 3: 13–15, 17–19**

This passage is part of Peter's sermon in the Temple. The continuity of the Church with the old Israel is brought out by the use of Old Testament titles for God. There follows a summary of the passion of Jesus in which ancient messianic titles are used. Peter contrasts the fact that the Jews chose a murderer to be reprieved, while the Just

One they condemned to death. But God raised Jesus from the dead, a fact to which the apostles were witnesses. However, Peter softens his account by asserting that the Jews acted through ignorance and that things had happened as God had foretold through his prophets. Now, therefore, is the time for repentance and conversion; a change of mind and conduct accompanied by penance, the motive for which is contained in the rest of the discourse.

Responsorial Psalm   4

℟ *Lift up the light of your face on us, O Lord.*
  or *Alleluia!*

1 When I call, answer me, O God of justice;
  from anguish you released me, have mercy and hear me! (R)

2 It is the Lord who grants favours to those whom he loves;
  the Lord hears me whenever I call him. (R)

3 'What can bring us happiness?' many say.
  Lift up the light of your face on us, O Lord. (R)

4 I will lie down in peace and sleep comes at once,
  for you alone, Lord, make me dwell in safety. (R)

In this Psalm of trust, which belongs to the individual laments (cf. p. 12), the expression of confidence dominates. This confidence is based on previous benefits or saving acts of God which the psalmist has experienced in a personal and intimate way.

Second Reading   1 John 2: 1–5

John tells his readers that Jesus is the sacrifice that takes our sins away. Thus it is the propitiatory quality of Christ's death that he emphasizes. The greatest weapon against sin is the recognition of it and a dependence on the redemption brought about by Jesus Christ. At this point in his letter John brings in and emphasizes the theme of keeping the commandments in order to 'know' God. (In Hebrew thought the word for 'knowing' implies *intimate knowledge*.) Indeed, love for God is manifested through obedience to the commandments, and to the one who does obey the commandments, 'God's love comes to perfection in him'.

Gospel   **Luke 24: 35–48**

The passage describes Jesus' appearance to his disciples, and bears some resemblance to John's account (see last Sunday). The reaction to Jesus' presence shows that the acceptance of the resurrection rests on faith and not on divine apparitions or previous announcements of Jesus. However, Jesus shows the marks of his wounds, and, on touching him and discovering that it really is him, 'they disbelieved for joy' (as is the literal translation of the Greek). The final few verses are found only in Luke's account and show the origin of apostolic preaching and tradition. There is insistence on the fact that Jesus must suffer and rise again. Indeed, the passion narrative received its formulation very early on in the infant Church. And it must be remembered that the apostles were not simply witnesses but men possessed by the Spirit, and as such, became the foundation of the Church which rests on Christ.

Fourth Sunday of Easter

First Reading   **Acts 4: 8–12**

Here we have Peter's first discourse before the Sanhedrin (the supreme Council of the Jews) – or, at any rate, a summary of it. It differs from his other discourses (e.g. Acts 3: 12ff., see p. 75) in that there is no call to repentance. Peter makes reference to the miracle which eventually brought about his and John's arrest. And in explaining that the healing was brought about in the name of Jesus, he goes on to point out that it was through the very man that the Jewish authorities had had crucified. The antithesis is brought out with reference to the Old Testament. The stone that they rejected (namely, Jesus) has now become the keystone of the New Order. Only through him will men be saved.

Responsorial Psalm   **118 (117)**

℞ *The stone which the builders rejected*
   has become the corner stone.
   or *Alleluia!*

1 Alleluia!
  Give thanks to the Lord for he is good,
  for his love has no end.
  It is better to take refuge in the Lord
  than to trust in men:
  it is better to take refuge in the Lord
  than to trust in princes. (R)

2 I will thank you for you have given answer
  and you are my saviour.
  The stone which the builders rejected
  has become the corner stone.
  This is the work of the Lord,
  a marvel in our eyes. (R)

3 Blessed in the name of the Lord
  is he who comes.
  We bless you from the house of the Lord
  I will thank you for you have given answer
  and you are my saviour.
  Give thanks to the Lord for he is good;
  for his love has no end. (R)

A hymn (cf. p. 12), this Psalm is the last of the 'Hallel' group
(Psalms 113–118), a sequence of praise sung in the Temple at
the major festivals. It connects with the first reading through the
metaphor of the 'stone', which is taken, indeed, from here.

Second Reading   **1 John 3: 1–2**

The source of sanctification for the Christian is the love of God. This
love of God has been 'lavished upon us' through the Sonship of
Christ, the incarnate love of God, who gave himself up to death for
us. 'The world', on the other hand, is incapable of knowing the
children because it does not know God. At the return of Jesus, the
natural Son of God, the adopted children will see the resemblance

more closely because then 'we shall be like him, because we shall see him as he really is'.

Gospel **John 10: 11–18**

The preceding chapters have spoken of Jesus as the light of the world, and chapter 10 introduces two comparisons: Jesus the gate, and this present image of Jesus the shepherd. He now refers to himself explicitly as 'good', that is, as the true, perfect shepherd of whom he has been speaking. He, of course, will lay down his life in a far more significant way than the shepherd of whom he speaks. Jesus lays down his life for the sheep of God (see John 15: 13). In this he contrasts sharply with the Pharisees, the hired helpers, who have no real interest in or personal concern for the sheep. The mutual knowledge of shepherd and sheep is, in turn, an extension of the mutual knowledge of the Father and the Son. It is this mutual knowledge of Father and Son that explains the supreme sacrifice, and explains, moreover, the love of the Father for the Son. For the sacrifice of the Son is performed in harmony with the will of the Father. Indeed, it is this freedom of Christ's obedience which is the condition of the efficacy of his work.

Fifth Sunday of Easter

First Reading **Acts 9: 26–31**

This is the account of Saul's (Paul's) first visit to Jerusalem (Acts records six different visits of Saul to this city after his conversion). Remembering Saul's former attitude towards the Christians, the disciples were obviously apprehensive. Thus Barnabas became mediator between the former persecutor of the Church and the apostles. Luke records nothing of the topic of the discussion, mentioned in Galatians 1: 18–20 (which clearly refers to the same visit). Saul is presented as an individual to whom the Lord has spoken. That he was accepted is shown by the fact that he went around 'preaching fearlessly in the name of the Lord'. The 'Hellenists' are most likely Jews who spoke only Greek. That the 'brothers' took him away from trouble is another pointer to his acceptance. The final verse is another minor summary, and explicitly mentions the spread of the Church to Judea, Galilee and Samaria (see the commission in Acts 1: 8), and provides a transition to Peter's missionary journey (Acts 9: 32ff.).

Responsorial Psalm   22 (21)

℞ *You, Lord, are my praise in the great assembly.*
  or *Alleluia!*

1 My vows I will pay before those who fear him.
  The poor shall eat and shall have their fill.
  They shall praise the Lord, those who seek him.
  May their hearts live for ever and ever! (R)

2 All the earth shall remember and return to the Lord,
  all families of the nations worship before him.
  They shall worship him, all the mighty of the earth;
  before him shall bow all who go down to the dust. (R)

3 And my soul shall live for him, my children serve him.
  They shall tell of the Lord to generations yet to come,
  declare his faithfulness to peoples yet unborn:
  'These things the Lord has done.' (R)

This Psalm begins as an individual lament and ends as an individual thanksgiving. This sequence is common in the Psalms (e.g. Psalms 5, 13, 16). The verses here speak of God's work being always bound up with his purposes for all creation, with the concluding verses extending even further the outworkings of God's saving acts.

Second Reading   1 John 3: 18–24

The context of this passage tells us that love is the great sign of having passed out of the kingdom of Satan and of wrath. Jesus conquered death by laying down his life of his own free will and taking it up again. In this act we have the supreme example of love (see Romans 5: 6ff.). If we wish to follow Christ we, too, must love. But this love is practical, not merely theoretical; we must *practise* charity. In this way we can be assured that we are on the side of God. We need not be afraid because of our past sins, for God knows our weakness and, in his mercy, can forgive us. We have, therefore, grounds for confidence. And the greatest source for this confidence is obedience to the commandments – summed up as believing in Jesus and loving one another. Whoever keeps God's commandments 'lives in God and God lives in him'.

Gospel   John 15: 1–8

In this extended metaphor of the vine and the branches, the theme is the relationship of the Christian to Christ, the community of life that they share, of which Christ's life is the source. The figure of the vine and branches presupposes that the Christian life is essentially one of activity, of bearing fruit. One cannot be a passive Christian, because union with Christ is not only a condition for bearing fruit but, indeed, demands this. Anything other results in the breaking of this unity, like a dead branch, fit only for casting aside. Unity, however, brings with it efficacy of prayer, as well as the glorifying of the Father in the works of the Son's disciples.

Sixth Sunday of Easter

First Reading   Acts 10: 25–26, 34–35, 44–48

The whole of chapter 10 concerns the conversion of Cornelius, a Roman centurion. This event is of great importance because it set the precedent for the admission of Gentiles into the Church. Nor were the implications missed by the infant Church, as subsequent controversy shows. We pick up the story where Peter approaches the house of Cornelius and is treated as someone more than human. Peter refuses this obeisance: 'I am only a man after all'. The reading then moves on to the opening words of Peter's classic proclamation of the gospel. The discourse begins with a statement of the universality of salvation and proceeds with an account of Christ's life from his baptism to his resurrection. The descent of the Spirit 'on all the listeners' bears witness to the genuineness of the conversion. Peter recognizes this and 'gives orders for them to be baptized in the name of Jesus Christ'.

Responsorial Psalm   **98 (97)**

℟ *The Lord has shown his salvation to the nations.*
  or *Alleluia!*

1 Sing a new song to the Lord
  for he has worked wonders.
  His right hand and his holy arm
  have brought salvation. (R)

2 The Lord has made known his salvation;
  has shown his justice to the nations.
  He has remembered his truth and love
  for the house of Israel. (R)

3 All the ends of the earth have seen
  the salvation of our God.
  Shout to the Lord all the earth,
  ring out your joy. (R)

One of the enthronement hymns (cf. p. 13). It summons the faithful
to praise because of the new phase of their lives which is brought
about by the marvellous things done for them by God, their Creator
and Saviour. This work has now been fulfilled by the saving act of
Christ.

Second Reading   **1 John 4: 7–10**

John returns once more to the theme of love for one another. When
he states that 'God is love', he means that love characterizes God's
dealings with men. It was out of gratuitous love on God's part that he
sent his only Son as saviour and redeemer of mankind. This concept
of God's love is the unique possession of Christianity and the greatest
proof of its truth. The only requirement attached to the gift of love
given to us is that we share it with others. It is the love for others
whom we can see that brings us as close as we can come on earth to
the love of God whom we cannot see.

Gospel   **John 15: 9–17**

This reading is taken from the true-vine-and-branches speech of
Jesus, which is really a discourse on the relation of the Christian to

Christ (see last Sunday). The figure of the vine and branches which comes immediately before this reading in context, pre-supposes the Christian life to be one of activity, of bearing fruit. Union with Christ demands this fruit-bearing activity. Christian love has the model of the love of Christ himself, which, in turn, gives the Christian the ability to live up to this ideal. The final verses remind the disciples of the divine initiative which has been present throughout sacred history. Now the Son, sent by the Father, has chosen his own. And their life and mission, in turn, continue this work of divine grace.

Ascension Day

First Reading   Acts 1: 1–11

Luke begins the Acts of the Apostles by relating it to his Gospel. This first work ended with the command to preach to all nations and to await the descent of the Spirit in Jerusalem. During the forty days preceding the Ascension Jesus had often appeared to the apostles confirming their faith and instructing them concerning the spiritual kingdom that he was establishing. With v. 6 the scene changes, though it is not immediately apparent. They have moved from the meal, the scene of the opening verses, to the mount of Olives, where the apostles' question makes it clear that they still possess a confused idea of the nature of Christ's kingdom. And he does not correct this idea because that will be the work of the Holy Spirit. He simply enjoins on them the obligations of apostleship (v. 8). Then he returns to heaven. The cloud is the classic biblical sign of the divine presence. The *two* men perhaps are a reference to the procedural rule of two witnesses (for substantiation in law) made applicable in the Christian community (see Matthew 18: 15ff.; 1 Timothy 5: 19). It is a formula borrowed from Deuteronomy 19: 15. The two men announce Christ's return and so give basis for one of the great objects of Christian hope.

Responsorial Psalm   **47 (46)**

℟ *God goes up with shouts of joy;*
  the Lord goes up with trumpet blast.
  or *Alleluia!*

1 All peoples, clap your hands,
  cry to God with shouts of joy!
  For the Lord, the Most High, we must fear,
  great king over all the earth. (℟)

2 God goes up with shouts of joy;
  the Lord goes up with trumpet blast.
  Sing praise for God, sing praise,
  sing praise to our king, sing praise. (℟)

3 God is king of all the earth.
  Sing praise with all your skill.
  God is king over the nations;
  God reigns on his holy throne. (℟)

This Psalm is a hymn celebrating the enthronement of God. It
expresses the ultimate reality – God is the supreme, universal King.
The sentiments fit in with the theme of the Ascension, where Christ
returns in glory to the right hand of God in his kingdom.

Second Reading   **Ephesians 1: 17–23**

This reading brings out the connection between faith and love. Faith
is commitment to Christ. With this union comes an appreciation of
God's love for mankind manifested in his Son. This, in turn, is
shown by our love for one another. The knowledge that Paul speaks
of is not not merely conceptual knowledge, but a personal knowledge of God himself, an experience shown in the brotherhood of
men (both Jew and Gentile) previously divided by so many social
and racial barriers. The enthronement of Christ signifies that Jesus,
in his humanity, has now attained a position of equality and association with the Father whereby all God's power can act through him.
The resurrection, ascension and glorification of Jesus are seen as one
great, continuous act by the Father. By this act Christ has conquered
and is victorious. Nothing now stands in the way of God's plan for
men in Christ. Paul also sees the Church as the necessary comple-

ment of Christ. The two are an organic unity. Christ is the invisible, elevated leader and head of a visible world community.

Gospel   **Mark 16: 15–20**

Scholars think that Mark may in fact have ended his Gospel at 16: 8, though its abruptness suggests that the real ending has been lost. The reading is part of what is called the Canonical Ending (vv. 9–20), which may date to no earlier than the second century. Traditionally the ending is divided into four parts, the last two of which make up the reading here. The section opens with the appearance to the Eleven which forms a climax in this ending. The universal aspect of the command cannot be missed. The conditions for salvation are faith and baptism. And the proclamation of the good news will bring either (spiritual) life or death according to the response of belief or unbelief. 'He who believes' may refer to a baptismal confession. The last two verses recount the ascension (a fitting conclusion to the appearances recorded in this ending) and the beginning of the apostolic mission. The 'word' is none other than the gospel (good news) itself.

Seventh Sunday of Easter

First Reading   **Acts 1: 15–17, 20–26**

The incident related in this section of Acts seems to have little importance for subsequent history and, indeed, Matthias does not appear again. Why Luke included it is to be found in vv. 21–22, where Peter puts forward a theology of apostleship and of the foundation of the Church. A replacement for Judas must be found in order to bring the number of apostles back up to twelve. The apostolic college represents in the New Law what the twelve tribal leaders represented in the Old. The primary requirement for the replacement is that he must have been 'with us' from the Baptism to the Ascension. He would thus be able to bear witness to the Resurrection. This is the guarantee of authenticity to second generation Christianity and to the later Church.

Responsorial Psalm   **103 (102)**

℞ *The Lord has set his sway in heaven.*
    or *Alleluia!*

1 My soul, give thanks to the Lord,
   all my being, bless his holy name.
   My soul, give thanks to the Lord
   and never forget all his blessings. (R)

2 For as the heavens are high above the earth
   so strong is his love for those who fear him.
   As far as the east is from the west
   so far does he remove our sins. (R)

3 The Lord has set his sway in heaven
   and his kingdom is ruling over all.
   Give thanks to the Lord, all his angels,
   mighty in power, fulfilling his word. (R)

A festal hymn (cf. p. 12) calling for praise and describing the works of God and his ways. He is praised as the merciful Covenant-Lord and King of the universe. The eternal fidelity of God described is an apt reminder of what he has done through his Son's redeeming death and resurrection.

Second Reading   **1 John 4: 11–16**

God's love is his gratuitous gift to us, but it does entail one requirement and that is that we should share it with others. It is through love of those we can see that we manifest our love for God whom we cannot see. Perhaps this was an attack on those false teachers who claimed a special knowledge and vision of God. 'No one has ever seen God', says John, but we know that we live in him and he in us, because we share his Spirit which is the pledge of our union with God. John adds his own testimony to this fact through his witness that God sent his Son as Saviour to the world. Belief in him will bring us the love which means that God lives in us and we in him.

Gospel   **John 17: 11–19**

This passage is part of a longer section that since the sixteenth century has been called the 'High-priestly prayer', though equivalent expressions are to be found in the Fathers of the Church. It is an apt description because it is Christ's prayer consecrating his body and blood for the sacrifice that was about to be offered, and his blessing over the Church that he will bring to birth in his glorification. The occasion for the prayer stems from the fact that his disciples will need divine protection in a special way now that his visible presence is being taken from them. The unity of the Father and the Son is to be the model of their unity. Because 'the world' (that is the power of darkness and sin) hates the light, the Church that Christ leaves behind needs divine protection, for it is the Church's destiny to live in the world but not be of it, to affect it but not be affected by it. The final two verses complete the thought expressed. The apostolic mission is the same as Christ's mission from the Father. It is made holy in truth.

Pentecost Sunday

First Reading   **Acts 2: 1–11**

Luke here describes the events that took place on the day of Pentecost. Jewish tradition holds that the Law was given on this day, fifty days after the Passover. Luke's reference to it indicates that it is an important date in his history of the Church's formative past. It signals the starting-point for the new era of the Church which the Holy Spirit inaugurates. Moses returned with the gift of the Law. Jesus sends his gift of the Spirit. The 'powerful wind' and the 'fire' are elements associated with the appearance of God. As a direct result of this fulfilment of Christ's promise (1: 7), the disciples begin to speak according to the dictates of the Spirit. It is the Spirit which is the driving force in the proclamation of the message (2: 4). The speaking in tongues which is reported may well be an historically sound oral tradition referring to the first public proclamation of the gospel by the disciples amidst circumstances of frenzied enthusiasm and ecstatic speech that persuaded the hearers of the Spirit's involvement. The list of Jews from the Dispersion, in a more or less geographical sweep from east to west, is meant to represent the universality of mankind, recalling perhaps Jesus' command 'to be witnesses to the ends of the earth' (1: 8).

Responsorial Psalm 104 (103)

℟ *Send forth your Spirit, O Lord,*
  and renew the face of the earth.
  or *Alleluia!*

1 Bless the Lord, my soul!
  Lord God, how great you are,
  How many are your works, O Lord!
  The earth is full of your riches. (R)

2 You take back your spirit, they die,
  returning to the dust from which they came.
  You send forth your spirit, they are created;
  and you renew the face of the earth. (R)

3 May the glory of the Lord last for ever!
  May the Lord rejoice in his works!
  May my thoughts be pleasing to him.
  I find my joy in the Lord. (R)

A hymn to the Creator. The verses here summarize preceding tributes to God in a confession of total and constant dependence upon him. The reference to the Spirit is the obvious link with the first reading.

Second Reading **1 Corinthians 12: 3–7, 12–13**

Paul uses the term 'gifts' (Greek, *charismata*) in a wider sense than the technical theological use. For him it embraced all graces given primarily for the benefit of the Church. The many spiritual gifts all come from the one divine source, the Spirit, the Lord, the Father. The terms 'gifts', 'service', 'working' designate the spiritual gifts according to the different aspects we would associate with the Spirit, the Lord, and the Father. All these gifts manifest the Spirit's presence, and they have one purpose: the common good. Christ is *one* just as the body, though made up of many parts, is *one*. And it is baptism in the Spirit that incorporates the Christian into the risen, glorified body of Christ.

Gospel   **John 20: 19–23**

This is the first of two appearances to the disciples that make up John's conclusion to the history of the exaltation of Jesus. The evangelist's attention is still fixed on Easter Sunday, as the opening verse shows. After his greeting, repeated twice, Jesus transfers to his disciples his own mission. But this mission cannot be performed unaided. So now is the moment when the promise of the gift of the Spirit, dependent upon the exaltation and departure of Jesus (16: 7), can be fulfilled. It is the Spirit who produces the effect of the apostolic preaching in convicting the world of sin, righteousness and judgement. The twofold effect of remitting and retaining sins, in the final verse, is shown to be not arbitrary or fortuitous, but of absolute divine significance. It is part of the ministry of Christ that is perpetuated in the work of the Church and the Church's mission.

Trinity Sunday

First Reading   **Deuteronomy 4: 32–34, 39–40**

These verses are taken from a sermon on the election of Israel as the chosen people of God. It is one of the theologically high points of the whole book. The mighty deeds of the Lord in history, by which he chose and constituted Israel as his people, have demonstrated that he alone is God. A new element is added to the theological tradition: God's election of Israel was based upon his love for her. Israel's obedience, therefore, must be motivated by a responding love.

Responsorial Psalm   **33 (32)**

℟ *Happy the people the Lord has chosen as his own.*

1 The word of the Lord is faithful
   and all his works to be trusted.

The Lord loves justice and right
and fills the earth with his love. (R)

2 By his word the heavens were made,
   by the breath of his mouth all the stars.
   He spoke; and it came to be.
   He commanded; it sprang into being. (R)

3 The Lord looks on those who revere him,
   on those who hope in his love,
   to rescue their souls from death,
   to keep them alive in famine. (R)

4 Our soul is waiting for the Lord.
   The Lord is our help and our shield.
   May your love be upon us, O Lord,
   as we place all our hope in you. (R)

This Psalm is a good example of an Israelite hymn. It sets out the reasons for worshipping God, then passes on to consider the 'eye of the Lord'. Although in heaven, he is by no means remote from human affairs (as the first reading shows). The hymn draws to a close with a prayer. In fact the last two lines found their way into the Te Deum.

Second Reading   **Romans 8: 14–17**

This reading is taken from a longer section in which Paul tells us that through the Spirit the Christian becomes a child of God and is destined for glory. The vivifying power of the Spirit not only gives a man new life but makes him an adopted son and heir. Therefore the Christian is free and cannot possess the attitude of a slave. He is empowered by the Spirit to call upon God himself as Father. But Paul goes further still. The Christian, as an adopted son, is not only admitted into God's family, but also, by reason of this gratuitous gift of adoption, receives the right to become master of his adopted father's estate. Christ the true son already shares the Father's estate (i.e. glory); the Christian, as co-heir, is also destined to share it one day. Note the connection between sharing Christ's passion ('his sufferings') and sharing his resurrection.

Gospel   **Matthew 28: 16–20**

This passage occurs only in Matthew, and it concerns the apostolic commission. No mountain has previously been mentioned and no location need be sought. It lies in the same geographical order as the Mount of Temptation (4: 8), the Mount of the Sermon (5: 1), the Mount of the Transfiguration (17: 1). Matthew set his theologically significant events upon mountains. (In the Old Testament the 'mountain' was where God was to be found.) The commission is couched in terms of the experience of the early Church, and is a clear presentation of what the apostolic Church understood itself to be. By Christ's authority its makers may make disciples of all the nations. Their work is to baptize and teach. 'In(to) the name', signifies that the person baptized belongs to the trinity of Persons whose names are invoked in baptism. The final words are an assurance of the living presence of Jesus in the Church. The resurrection was the beginning of a new existence. The Church witnesses to the resurrection, for its life and activity are a constant reminder that Jesus lives.

Note on Sundays in Ordinary Time

The first Sunday in Ordinary Time is always the feast of the Baptism of the Lord. The other Sundays then fellow until Lent supervenes; the sequence begins again on the Sunday after Trinity Sunday. However, the sequence does not recommence exactly where it left off. (This gives the flexibility essential because years vary in their number of Sundays and in the position of Easter.) Either two or three Sundays are omitted in any one year. The table shows which these will be.

Sundays in Ordinary Time

Years	5	6	7	8	9	10	11
1982	7 Feb	14 Feb	21 Feb	—	—	—	13 Jun
1985	10 Feb	17 Feb	—	—	—	9 Jun	16 Jun
1988	7 Feb	14 Feb	—	—	—	5 Jun	12 Jun
1991	10 Feb	—	—	—	2 Jun	9 Jun	16 Jun
1994	6 Feb	13 Feb	—	—	—	5 Jun	12 Jun

Ordinary Time

Second Sunday in Ordinary Time

First Reading   1 Samuel 3: 3–10, 19

Eli, the priest of the sanctuary at Shiloh, hoped that his sons would succeed him. However, they abused their privileges as priests so much that God told Eli that his sons would die in battle. These were the days of the life-and-death struggle between Israel and the Philistines, when loyalty to God was paramount. Whenever human wickedness threatens God's plans, he is able to raise up new, faithful, servants. So it was with Samuel. Taught by Eli, he offered himself for divine service by repeating the prayer 'Speak; for thy servant hears'.

Responsorial Psalm   40 (39)

℞ *Here I am Lord!*
   I come to do your will.

1 I waited, I waited for the Lord
   and he stooped down to me;
   he heard my cry.
   He put a new song into my mouth,
   praise of our God. (R)

2 You do not ask for sacrifice and offerings,
   but an open ear.
   You do not ask for holocaust and victim.
   Instead, here am I. (R)

3 In the scroll of the book it stands written
   that I should do your will.
   My God, I delight in your law
   in the depth of my heart. (R)

4 Your justice I have proclaimed
   in the great assembly.
   My lips I have not sealed;
   you know it, O Lord. (R)

In this individual prayer for deliverance (cf. p. 12), the psalmist proclaims, like Samuel, the need for a listening ear. He adds also the need for joyous proclamation of God's mercies.

Second Reading   **1 Corinthians 6: 13–15, 17–20**

Paul appears to be arguing here against sexual immortality. Some Corinthian Christians reasoned that if Christians could eat whatever food they liked, they could also use their bodies immorally without offending God. Paul's reply is, in effect, that the word 'body' has one sense when it comes to eating food, and quite a different sense where sex is concerned. In this latter sense, 'body' includes the mental and spiritual powers of a person, as well as the physical powers, all of which are to be given unreservedly to the Lord's service. This is because Christians have been rescued from slavery to sin by the Lord's costly sacrifice, and have received the indwelling power of the Holy Spirit.

Gospel   **John 1: 35–42**

The most important Old Testament sacrifices for sin involved not a lamb, but a bullock or a goat. A lamb was killed and eaten at the Passover, but there is only slight evidence that this lamb was thought of as a sin-bearer. John the Baptist's designation of Jesus as 'Lamb of God' thus implied a new and profound interpretation of the Old Testament. The death of Jesus inaugurates the New Covenant, and his shed blood atones for sin. But the image of the lamb, referring back to Isaiah 53: 7, conveys the sense of the humble obedience to the divine will undertaken by Jesus. The title 'Lamb of God' would have meant little to the earliest disciples until after the Resurrection; but such was the hope that Jesus could inspire, that three ordinary men were led to pledge their obedience to his service, including Peter, whose new name (a rock) came from the Lord himself.

Third Sunday in Ordinary Time

First Reading   **Jonah 3: 1–5, 10**

The book of Jonah is remarkable in the way that it brings together and emphasizes teachings that can be found elsewhere, but not prominently, in the Old Testament. God is presented as one who is concerned in the affairs of a non-Israelite nation; Jonah is presented as an exclusivist, who would deny God's right to deal with other nations. The promptness with which the Ninevites respond to the prophet's proclamation of judgement contrasts vividly with the lack of response by the Israelites to similar warnings, given many times in the Old Testament. Further, God's graciousness is shown in his decision to stay the judgement in the face of the genuine repentance of the people of Nineveh. The passage is a warning not to make God fit into *our* expectations of what he should or should not do.

Responsorial Psalm   25 (24)

℟ *Lord, make me know your ways.*

1 Lord, make me know your ways.
   Lord, teach me your paths.
   Make me walk in your truth, and teach me:
   for you are God my saviour. (R)

2 Remember your mercy, Lord,
   and the love you have shown from of old.
   In your love remember me,
   because of your goodness, O Lord. (R)

3 The Lord is good and upright.
   He shows the path to those who stray.
   He guides the humble in the right path;
   he teaches his way to the poor. (R)

This prayer of an individual asks that God will always assist us to follow his truth and his love, and affirms his graciousness to all who are sincere.

Second Reading   1 Corinthians 7: 29–31

It was commonly believed by the earliest disciples that the kingdom inaugurated by the death and resurrection of Jesus would shortly be consummated, at which point the present world would pass away. It is from this perspective that Paul gives advice to husbands, mourners, those who rejoice, and those engaging in business. He does not advise them to suspend these activities. They are to engage in them as people who know that this present world is not the sum total of reality, but that it gets its true meaning from the unseen world which

97

is glimpsed through God's revelation. It should be no different for Christians today. We have lost the sense of living in a world that is shortly to end – although the threat of nuclear disasters makes this a physical possibility – but we should not have lost the sense that all our actions are to be placed in the context of eternity.

Gospel   **Mark 1: 14–20**

The first public preaching of Jesus took place in Galilee after the arrest of John the Baptist, and was a call to repentance (turning, or re-turning to God) because 'the Kingdom of God has drawn near'. The 'Kingdom of God' means God exerting his sovereignty on earth in a new and more direct manner. But what is meant by 'has drawn near'? It is more than 'just around the corner' and less than 'has arrived fully without remainder'. In Jesus, God is exercising his sovereignty in a new way, and he continues to do this through the witness of his Church; yet there is a hiddenness about the presence of the Kingdom in Jesus. That hiddenness will one day give place to full manifestation. Meanwhile, we follow the earliest disciples in faith and hope, as we respond to the call 'Follow me!'

Fourth Sunday in Ordinary Time

First Reading   **Deuteronomy 18: 15–20**

It is clear from the Old Testament that there were prophets who were outwardly prophets, but whose words did not come from God (see Jeremiah 28). This reading both issues the strongest possible warning to such prophets, and also gives hope to Israel that God will raise up a prophet like Moses. In Old Testament tradition, Moses is not the first of the prophets (Abraham is so entitled at Genesis 20: 7); but he is the greatest, because he talked with God 'face to face' (Exodus 33: 11). Thus the prophet referred to in this reading will be a prophet extraordinary, interpreting to God's people the deepest aspects of divine truth.

Responsorial Psalm   **95 (94)**

℞ *O that today you would listen to his voice!*
   Harden not your hearts.

1 Come, ring out our joy to the Lord;
  hail the rock who saves us.
  Let us come before him, giving thanks,
  with songs let us hail the Lord. (R)

2 Come in; let us kneel and bend low;
  let us kneel before the God who made us
  for he is our God and we
  the people who belong to his pasture,
  the flock that is led by his hand. (R)

3 O that today you would listen to his voice!
  'Harden not your hearts as at Meribah,
  as on that day at Massah in the desert
  when your fathers put me to the test;
  when they tried me, though they saw my work.' (R)

In a Psalm of communal thanksgiving (cf. p. 12) celebrating the
kingship of God, God is praised not only as creator, but also as
Israel's redeemer; and this latter fact carries the obligation of obedience.

Second Reading   **1 Corinthians 7: 32–35**

Paul, unlike false prophets, is well aware of the difference between
his own advice, and commandments that he has received from the
Lord (see vv. 25–6 of this chapter). Here, he gives his advice to the
unmarried and the married. They should stay as they are in view of
the imminent end of the present world (v. 26). The unmarried can
give their whole attention to the service of God. The married have a
divine duty to their spouses in addition. The one state is not necessarily
superior to the other; each has its proper office and functions.
And Christians today must find out in which state they can best serve
God.

Gospel   **Mark 1: 21–28**

The Jews in the first century entertained several 'messianic' hopes (see John 1: 19–23), of which one was the hope that God would raise up a prophet like Moses. Jesus fulfils this hope, as he fulfils the other hopes. The people were amazed because Jesus spoke with an authority unlike that of the scribes. The latter were concerned to interpret what had been handed down by the fathers. Jesus spoke with the authority of his certainty of a divine mission. In the Sermon on the Mount he went so far as to extend and challenge the Mosaic law in some points (see Matthew 5: 27–48). The words and works of Jesus are thus signs of God's new and final intervention in the world for its salvation.

Fifth Sunday in Ordinary Time

First Reading   **Job 7: 1–4, 6–7**

Out of the depths of illness and despair, Job likens human existence to the life of a slave or a casual worker. There is nothing to look forward to, and, in any case, life is short. It might be supposed that this is an irreligious attitude on the part of Job; but on the contrary, such honesty is part of Job's determination to maintain his integrity, and not to accept the unconvincing arguments by which his friends explain his misfortune. To be aware of human insignificance and weakness is to possess a profound religious sense.

Responsorial Psalm   **147 (146)**

℟ *Praise the Lord who heals the broken-hearted*
  or *Alleluia!*

1 Alleluia!
  Praise the Lord for he is good;
  sing to our God for he is loving:
  to him our praise is due. (R)

2 The Lord builds up Jerusalem
  and brings back Israel's exiles,

he heals the broken-hearted,
he binds up all their wounds.
He fixes the number of the stars;
he calls each one by its name. (R)

3 Our Lord is great and almighty;
his wisdom can never be measured.
The Lord raises the lowly;
he humbles the wicked to the dust. (R)

This communal hymn of praise declares God's special concern for
the weak and the lowly.

Second Reading   1 Corinthians 9: 16–19, 22–23

Some of the Corinthian Christians had cast doubts upon Paul's
authority as an apostle. One ground for this doubt was that Paul,
unlike other apostles, had not expected the Corinthians to support
him financially. In the earlier part of this chapter, Paul does not deny
that apostles have a right to be financially supported. He goes on to
assert, however, that where the gospel is concerned, an apostle must
consider waiving his rights if the work of salvation will be furthered
as a result. The gospel is not a human possession, it is entrusted to
the apostle; and the greatest reward is to see the gospel accepted.
Thus Paul is prepared to waive many of the things that he would
personally prefer, so as to enter into full sympathy with those to
whom he preaches.

Gospel   Mark 1: 29–39

We have here a picture, full of vitality, of the earliest days of the
Galilean ministry of Jesus. With so much feverish activity of healing
going on, it is hardly surprising that everyone was looking for Jesus.
The passage also points to a limitation of the earthly ministry of Jesus – it
was restricted to where he happened to be, and there must have been
many who were disappointed not to see or hear him. For what did he
pray on this occasion to his Father? Perhaps, at the very least, that
people would respond to the demands of his preaching, and would
not seek him simply as a healer.

Sixth Sunday in Ordinary Time

First Reading   Leviticus 13: 1–2, 45–46

The Hebrew word for 'leprosy' covered a wider range of ailments than what we today associate with leprosy, through leprosy missions. It is clear from Leviticus 13–14 that some forms of leprosy could disappear, and the leper be re-admitted to society. However, whether or not the disease contracted was a mild or an incurable skin complaint, the certified leper had to withdraw from society, and live as an outcast, dependent on the gifts that were left for him.

Responsorial Psalm   32 (31)

℟ *You are my hiding place, O Lord;*
   you surround me with cries of deliverance.

1 Happy the man whose offence is forgiven,
   whose sin is remitted.
   O happy the man to whom the Lord
   imputes no guilt,
   in whose spirit is no guile. (R)

2 But now I have acknowledged my sins;
   my guilt I did not hide.
   I said: 'I will confess
   my offence to the Lord.'
   And you, Lord have forgiven
   the guilt of my sin. (R)

3 Rejoice, rejoice in the Lord,
   exult, you just!
   O come, ring out your joy,
   all you upright of heart. (R)

This Psalm of thanksgiving for forgiveness expresses God's graciousness to those who hide nothing from him.

Second Reading   1 Corinthians 10: 31–11: 1

No early Christian did more than Paul to emphasize that the gospel breaks down human barriers and brings freedom. Distinctions between Jews and non-Jews, between ritually 'clean' and 'unclean' foods are swept away. At the same time, a Christian must on occasion forgo his liberty, if to insist on it would lead to alienating others from the gospel. In such cases, the guiding maxim must be to do that which will bring the greatest glory to God, especially the saving of non-believers.

Gospel   **Mark 1: 40–45**

There was no need for Jesus actually to touch the leper who came to him; Jesus could have healed him from a distance. By touching him, he showed how the active grace of God goes to lengths that humans would regard as unnecessary or even dangerous. Early manuscript tradition is divided over whether Jesus was moved with compassion or moved with anger at the leper's request. If the correct reading is anger, then perhaps Jesus was angry with the implication in the leper's request, that Jesus might not want to heal him. The leper would be so used to being treated as an outcast by others, that he might doubt Jesus's willingness to help. Jesus' anger would then be directed at that human behaviour that had undermined the leper's confidence. Thank God that his grace takes risks where human attitudes play safe.

Seventh Sunday in Ordinary Time

First Reading   **Isaiah 43: 18–19, 21–22, 24–25**

The prophet of the time of the exile in Babylon (587–539) addresses a people who have begun to doubt whether there is any more point in turning to God. The prophet declares that God is about to deliver his people, just as he delivered them at the Exodus. As God's people, they must be holy; and this they can only become by returning to their God, in whom is abundant mercy to forgive sins.

Responsorial Psalm   **41 (40)**

℟ *Heal my soul for I have sinned against you.*

1 Happy the man who considers the poor and the weak.
  The Lord will save him in the day of evil,

will guard him, give him life, make him happy in the land
and will not give him up to the will of his foes. (R)

2 The Lord will help him on his bed of pain,
he will bring him back from sickness to health.
As for me, I said: 'Lord, have mercy on me.
heal my soul for I have sinned against you.' (R)

3 If you uphold me I shall be unharmed
and set in your presence for evermore.
Blessed be the Lord, the God of Israel
from age to age. Amen. Amen. (R)

An individual prayer for deliverance in which the psalmist stresses
his need for divine forgiveness, the Psalm is confident in face of pain
and longs for God's presence.

Second Reading **2 Corinthians 1: 18–22**

Paul had been accused by the Corinthians of vacillation, saying 'Yes'
one moment and 'No' the next. Now he affirms that, whatever they
may think of him, there is certainly no vacillation in the Jesus Christ
he had preached to the Corinthians. Far from it! Through Christ
God had provided his great affirmation of mankind (one big 'Yes'!).
In our 'Amen' (which means 'truth' and so expresses an affirmation)
we say our 'Yes' to God who, through Christ, says 'Yes' to us.

Gospel **Mark 2: 1–12**

The friends of the paralytic thought that they knew what the paralytic needed most – physical healing. Jesus knew better; and his first
words, on the basis of the faith of the man's friends, were 'Your sins
are forgiven'. Jesus was running two risks in thus speaking: that he
would be accused of blasphemy, and that in any case, no one would
believe that the man's sins had been forgiven. To anticipate the
second danger, Jesus healed the paralytic, thus laying himself open
even further to the charge of blasphemy. But there was no alternative. The Son of Man is no mere deputy for God. It is his office so to
deal with sins that the sinner knows that he has been forgiven by God

himself. When Christians today make this same discovery, they begin to know who Jesus is.

Eighth Sunday in Ordinary Time

First Reading   Hosea 2: 16–17, 21–22

The relationship between a husband and his bride is used by some of the prophets to illustrate the relationship between God and his chosen people. Unfortunately, it is often necessary for Israel to be spoken of as an unfaithful bride who goes after other husbands. It is a common view today that so long as a person has some sort of religion, it does not matter which. This was not how the prophets saw the matter. When Israel turned to other gods (the Baals), the outcome was invariably the oppression of the weak by the strong, and the suppression of justice. Hosea looks forward to Israel's return to her true God, and to the peace and prosperity that will result.

Responsorial Psalm   103 (102)

℟ *The Lord is compassion and love.*

1 My soul, give thanks to the Lord,
   all my being, bless his holy name.
   My soul, give thanks to the Lord
   and never forget all his blessings. (R)

2 It is he who forgives all your guilt,
   who heals every one of your ills,
   who redeems your life from the grave,
   who crowns you with love and compassion. (R)

3 The Lord is compassion and love,
   slow to anger and rich in mercy.
   He does not treat us according to our sins
   nor repay us according to our faults. (R)

4 As far as the east is from the west
   so far does he remove our sins.
   As a father has compassion on his sons.
   The Lord has pity on those who fear him. (R)

This communal Psalm of thanksgiving affirms that God alone is the source of all true happiness, joy and mercy.

Second Reading   **2 Corinthians 3: 1–6**

Paul's opponents at Corinth, who were here possibly 'Judaizers' (people who argued that Christians must fully observe the Law of Moses), seem to have accused Paul of boasting as he sought to exercise his apostolic authority in the Christian Church. Paul replies that although he needs no letters of introduction, such a letter exists which can be read by all: the fruits of Christian discipleship among the Corinthians, fruits of Paul's labours in the gospel. Even so, Paul claims no credit for himself. All that he has achieved has been due to the enabling power of God, in the service of the gospel, centred in the person of Christ; this brings life and liberty, not slavish adherence to a written code.

Gospel   **Mark 2: 18–22**

The reply of Jesus to the question about fasting claims that, with his ministry, something quite new is happening. We do not know on which occasion the disciples of the Pharisees and of John the Baptist were fasting; but it must have been sufficiently important for people to notice the non-observance by the disciples of Jesus. By implying that he was the bridegroom, Jesus was probably making a messianic claim, whether or not the listeners realized this. The illustrations of the cloth and the wineskins, however, make it clear that the old order has been invaded by a new order, which the old order cannot contain. What is demanded is a radical response to the new order manifested in Jesus.

Ninth Sunday in Ordinary Time

First Reading   **Deuteronomy 5: 12–15**

The reason given in this reading for the observance of the sabbath (see the different reason at Exodus 20:11) is that it is to be a reminder of the slavery in Egypt from which God delivered Israel. It is noteworthy how the commandment stresses that the whole household is covered by the law. Masters are not to relax at the expense of their humblest servants. All must observe the sabbath, because all were the objects of God's saving action. When God saves his people, he does not divide them according to their class. The idea that time should be broken up into units of seven days, of which one should be a day of rest, appears to be a unique gift of the Hebrew people to mankind.

Responsorial Psalm 81 (80)

℟ *Ring out your joy to God our strength.*

1 Raise a song and sound the timbrel,
   the sweet-sounding harp and the lute,
   blow the trumpet at the new moon,
   when the moon is full, on our feast. (R)

2 For this is Israel's law,
   a command of the God of Jacob.
   He imposed it as a rule on Joseph,
   when he went out against the land of Egypt. (R)

3 A voice I did not know said to me:
   'I freed your shoulder from the burden;
   your hands were freed from the load.
   You called in distress and I saved you. (R)

4 'Let there be no foreign god among you,
   no worship of an alien god.
   I am the Lord your God,
   who brought you from the land of Egypt.' (R)

This communal hymn of praise (cf. p. 12), possibly used at the autumn feast of Tabernacles, reminds Israel of their deliverance from slavery in Egypt, and of the law which they are to obey in gratitude.

Second Reading 2 Corinthians 4: 6–11

2 Corinthians 4 continues from chapter 3 the theme of the confidence and encouragement that Christians receive from God, as they serve

that gospel which is his gift. Because it comes from God and conveys his power, the gospel does not allow the things of mankind to remain as they are. Even the witnesses of the gospel are aware of their utter human frailty in serving the gospel, as they experience despair, persecution and affliction. But the death which their own ambitions and desires begin to experience, is a sign of the life of Christ in their lives.

Gospel   **Mark 2: 23–3: 6**

Jesus is here presented in two conflicts with the religious leaders of his day concerning sabbath observance. In the case of the healing on the sabbath, the opponents of Jesus were not against the healing as such. Their point would be that since the man's life was not in danger, the healing should be deferred to a day other than the sabbath. In both his replies, Jesus not only challenges the widely-accepted interpretation of the sabbath law; he makes implicit messianic claims. Human interpretation of God's law cannot block the new manifestation of God's grace in Jesus. The sabbath law was meant to be a response to God's salvation of his people at the Exodus. It had become a hindrance to their liberty and healing.

Tenth Sunday in Ordinary Time

First Reading   **Genesis 3: 9–15**

Into this symbolic story about earliest man, the biblical writer concentrated and distilled much that had been learned from the history of God's encounters with Israel. The root problem of man's alienation from God was seen to be his disobedience – his desire to usurp God's place in the universe. Yet this disobedience was also a willing response to the power of evil outside of man, symbolized in this story by the serpent. In God's curse on the serpent is the hope of man's deliverance from evil. The phrase about the woman's seed bruising the serpent's head has traditionally been understood by Christians to be a reference to Christ.

Responsorial Psalm   130 (129)

℞ *With the Lord there is mercy and fullness of redemption.*

1 Out of the depths I cry to you, O Lord.
  Lord, hear my voice!
  O let your ears be attentive
  to the voice of my pleading. (R)

2 If you, O Lord, should mark our guilt,
  Lord, who would survive?
  But with you is found forgiveness:
  for this we revere you. (R)

3 My soul is waiting for the Lord,
  I count on his word.
  My soul is longing for the Lord
  more than watchman for daybreak. (R)

4 Because with the Lord there is mercy
  and fullness of redemption,
  Israel indeed he will redeem
  from all its iniquity. (R)

This individual prayer in time of distress falls into two parts. The darkness of the first part gives way to the hope of the second part, wonderfully expressing the paradox of the sinner whose hope of redemption is in God.

Second Reading   2 Corinthians 4: 13–5: 1

Paul here draws encouragement from the Old Testament as he considers the trials of witnessing to the gospel. We do not know which numbering system of the Psalms he was using; this is either 115: 1 in the Greek numbering or 116: 10 in the Hebrew. If it was the latter, he was citing a Psalm which celebrates deliverance by God from the power of death. Drawing on the encouragement of the feeling of solidarity with God's witnesses of old, he repeats his determination to speak out for God. He is strengthened by the hope of resurrection in Jesus, and by the certainty that the more he speaks, the more will his listeners respond to the gospel.

Gospel   **Mark 3: 20–35**

In the time of Jesus, belief in the reality of evil had taken the form of belief in a kingdom of wicked angels, whose chief was called Beelzebul and Satan, among other names. The healings and the exorcising of demons by Jesus are presented in the Gospels as the kingdom of God overcoming the kingdom of Satan. There were some, however, who attributed the power of Jesus to an alliance with the demonic, and this led to a powerful rebuff by Jesus. If Jesus is in league with Satan, then there is civil war in Satan's kingdom – which is impossible. Satan's kingdom in fact is being defeated because it is being overcome by one who is stronger; and to think otherwise is to sin against the Holy Spirit. This sin is unforgivable because it attributes to Satan what in fact is coming from God. There can be no forgiveness until the true and only source of forgiveness is humbly and gladly acknowledged.

Eleventh Sunday in Ordinary Time

First Reading   **Ezekiel 17: 22–24**

In the first part of Ezekiel 17, the prophet sets forth the allegory of the two eagles and the vine that was planted in Jerusalem. The interpretation of the allegory concerns the deeds of human rulers. One eagle, Nebuchadnezzar king of Babylon, had exiled the king of Judah to Babylon in 597 BC, and had replaced him in Jerusalem with a vine (the king's uncle, Zedekiah). But now the vine is seeking help from another eagle, the king of Egypt, and the prophet asserts that this alliance will produce only disaster. In today's reading, the prophet goes on to describe what God is to plant in Jerusalem – a discreet sprig of cedar that will become a mighty tree. This planting will succeed because it is God's planting. He alone can establish the kingdom that will endure for ever.

Responsorial Psalm   **92 (91)**

℟ *It is good to give you thanks, O Lord.*

1 It is good to give thanks to the Lord
   to make music to your name, O Most High,
   to proclaim your love in the morning
   and your truth in the watches of the night. (R)

2 The just will flourish like the palm-tree
   and grow like a Lebanon cedar. (R)

3 Planted in the house of the Lord
   they will flourish in the courts of our God,
   still bearing fruit when they are old,
   still full of sap, still green,
   to proclaim that the Lord is just.
   In him, my rock, there is no wrong. (R)

This hymn praises God for his just government of the world, and for the reward that he brings to his people who serve him faithfully.

Second Reading   **2 Corinthians 5: 6–10**

Paul has a profound sense of the way in which his destiny is bound up with Christ. Life on earth means fellowship with Christ, albeit fellowship dependent upon faith and not upon sight. At death, the limitations of the senses will be stripped away, and the Christian will be truly 'at home' with the Lord. This being 'at home' will involve being judged by Christ; but for the person who is already in fellowship with Christ in this life, it will not be judgement by a total stranger.

Gospel   **Mark 4: 26–34**

The parables of the Seed Growing Secretly and the Mustard Seed recall the reading from Ezekiel 17. Here, as there, it is emphasized that whatever man may do, the powers that produce the growth (i.e. establish and confirm the Kingdom of God) belong to God alone, and therefore cannot be overthrown by man. This passage envisages human co-operation in the growth of the Kingdom, although only God can bring success from what man plants. The hiddenness of the

Kingdom is also implied. The mustard has its small beginnings in the work of a Galilean workman and his tiny band of disciples.

Twelfth Sunday in Ordinary Time

First Reading   Job 38: 1, 8–11

To understand the Old Testament attitude to nature, it must be remembered that the land of the Bible has a different climate from northern Europe. The winter season (approx. October–March) is a wet season, with the remainder of the year dry. We learn from the Bible that there were often famines caused by droughts. When rains eventually broke the droughts, they often did great damage – as in the parable of the wise and foolish builders (Matthew 7: 24–7). For the Israelites, storm and sea were manifestations of terrifying power which reminded them of their insignificance. Yet they also believed that God was mightier than these awesome displays of power, and in them, they sensed his incomparability.

Responsorial Psalm   107 (106)

℟ *O give thanks to the Lord,*
   for his love endures for ever.
   or *Alleluia!*

1 Some sailed to the sea in ships
   to trade on the mighty waters.
   These men have seen the Lord's deeds,
   the wonders he does in the deep. (R)

2 For he spoke; he summoned the gale,
   tossing the waves of the sea
   up to heaven and back into the deep;
   their soul melted away in their distress. (R)

3 Then they cried to the Lord in their need
   and he rescued them from their distress.
   He stilled the storm to a whisper:
   all the waves of the sea were hushed. (R)

4 They rejoiced because of the calm
    and he led them to the haven they desired.
  Let them thank the Lord for his love,
    the wonders he does for men. (R)

A communal hymn of praise for God's deliverance from various types of danger here affirms God's control of the seas.

Second Reading   **2 Corinthians 5: 14–17**

The death of Christ is for Paul such a revolutionary event that it totally alters the way in which he regards himself and his fellow men. The love of God in Christ is a love that confers value on the worthless. Where this is acknowledged and accepted, there follows death to self, and life for Christ. Other Christians are no longer regarded as they were before. They are then to be seen according to the new value which has been placed upon them by Christ.

Gospel   **Mark 4: 35–41**

The miracle of the stilling of the storm ought, in view of the Old Testament background including that in the First Reading and the Psalm, to have convinced the disciples who Jesus was. However, the idea that God should be incarnate was utterly foreign to them. This sign could be only a part of their preparation for understanding the truth. The Sea of Galilee, which they were crossing, is 600 feet below sea-level, and surrounded by hills 1,500 to 3,500 feet high. Winds sweeping down from these hills can make the sea boil like a cauldron. But it is likely that Jesus did not perform the miracle gladly. His rebuke to the disciples about their lack of faith amounted to this: you knew that I was with you in the boat and that therefore nothing could harm you. Why did you waken me? why did you not trust? Mark's readers are therefore reminded that the power of God is just as much available when unspectacular trust is present, as when we seek for unusual and spectacular demonstrations of the divine.

Thirteenth Sunday in Ordinary Time

God created man for immortality. He is the only source of life; and by the supreme gift of himself he has given us eternal life.

First Reading **Wisdom 1: 13–15; 2: 23–24**

These verses from the Book of Wisdom are a kind of commentary on the stories of the Creation and Fall in Genesis 1–3, drawing out their implications in terms of eternal life. Since everything which God made was good (compare Genesis 1: 31) and death formed no part of his plan, man must from the first have been destined for immortality. Death entered the world through the agency of the Devil (Genesis 3) and the unrighteous follow him along the path to eternal death. But since we are made in God's image (Genesis 1: 27) we can avoid this fate through the practice of righteousness, which is by nature immortal, and so obtain eternal life.

Responsorial Psalm **30 (29)**

℟ *I will praise you, Lord, you have rescued me.*

1 I will praise you, Lord, you have rescued me
  and have not let my enemies rejoice over me.
  O Lord, you have raised my soul from the dead,
  restored me to life from those who sink into the grave. (R)

2 Sing psalms to the Lord, you who love him,
  give thanks to his holy name.
  His anger lasts but a moment; his favour through life,
  At night there are tears, but joy comes with dawn. (R)

3 The Lord listened and had pity.
  The Lord came to my help.
  For me you have changed my mourning into dancing,
  O Lord my God, I will thank you for ever. (R)

This Psalm is a song of praise (see p. 12) in which the psalmist thanks God for rescuing him from death and restoring him to a life of joy and hope.

Second Reading   **2 Corinthians 8: 7, 9, 13–15**

Paul is here trying to persuade the Christians at Corinth to be generous in their support of his appeal for money to help the impoverished Christians of Jerusalem. He asks them to match their other Christian virtues with their financial generosity, and sets before them the example of Jesus Christ himself. Although nothing can approach the generosity of Jesus, who unstintingly accepted the 'poverty' of suffering humanity so that men and women might become the children of God, his is the example we ought to follow. Finally Paul sets before his readers the ideal of mutuality in the Christian life: each is to supply the wants of others. The final quotation from Exodus 16: 18 makes the point that God provides a sufficiency for all his people if only they are ready to distribute his gifts equitably among themselves.

Gospel   **Mark 5: 21–43**

In these two stories Jesus is portrayed as the one who has power over life and death, sickness and health. These stories of the healing miracles of Jesus imply more than they describe. Jesus' cure of the chronically sick woman and his bringing back to life of Jairus' daughter were remembered by the Church and recorded in the Gospels not only because they illustrate his power to restore ordinary physical life but because the power over death and disease which they manifest has an even deeper implication: such complete power can be found only in one who is himself the creator and giver of life. These miracles consequently present the reader with a portrait of Jesus as the one in whose power it lies to give not only physical life but eternal life as well.

At the same time it is made clear that the gift of life can only be appropriated by those who have a personal faith in Jesus. The faith of the sick woman is such that she is healed simply by touching his robe. In the story of Jairus' daughter the need for faith is again a dominant feature. The girl's father and family already believe that Jesus is able to cure the sick, but to bring the dead back to life is another matter. But to the giver of life and to those who believe in him death is no more than sleep.

Fourteenth Sunday in Ordinary Time

The qualifications for God's service: confidence, humility, faith.

First Reading   Ezekiel 2: 2–5

Ezekiel had been deported with other Jews to Babylonia when Jerusalem submitted to the army of Nebuchadnezzar in 597 BC (2 Kings 24: 10–16). While he was living there among his fellow Jews 'by the River Chebar' he had an extraordinary vision which he called 'the appearance of the likeness of the glory of the Lord'. He prostrated himself in awe; and then he found himself addressed as described in this passage. These words spoken to him by God constituted his call to be a prophet: to be God's messenger sent to his own people to communicate to them whatever God might wish to say to them. He is warned that his companions may be unwilling to listen. But he is to consider two things, which are in fact vital for any person who finds himself chosen by God for his service: he is to expect hardship and must not be afraid; and he is not to be disappointed by apparent failure, for even if his message falls on deaf ears, being God's word it will in some mysterious way achieve its purpose – its recipients will know that there has been a prophet among them, and they will be either saved or judged by that fact.

Responsorial Psalm   123 (122)

℟ *Our eyes are on the Lord*
  till he show us his mercy.

1 To you have I lifted up my eyes,
   you who dwell in the heavens:
   my eyes, like the eyes of slaves
   on the hand of their lords. (R)

2 Like the eyes of a servant
   on the hand of her mistress,
   so our eyes are on the Lord our God
   till he show us his mercy. (R)

3 Have mercy on us, Lord, have mercy.
   We are filled with contempt.

Indeed all too full is our soul
with the scorn of the rich,
with the proud man's disdain. (R)

This Psalm is a lament, though it is inconsistent in its use of 'I' and 'we' which usually mark off individual from communal laments (see p. 12). It is written out of distress but not despair, in an attitude of expectation that God's mercy, though delayed, will nevertheless eventually be manifested.

Second Reading   2 Corinthians 12: 7–10

Since Paul's previous visit to the Church in Corinth, which he had himself founded (see Acts 18) and since his earlier letter to it (1 Corinthians) attempts had been made to undermine his authority there and to change the nature of the faith which he had taught. In 2 Corinthians he was mainly concerned to repair the damage. In an attempt to restore his authority he reminded the Corinthian Christians of his credentials and qualifications. At the beginning of this chapter he had embarked upon the subject of visions and divine revelations which he had received. But then, in this passage, he uses himself as an object-lesson for those who might think themselves to be his superior. He describes how the Lord took steps to prevent him from thinking himself above earthly things: he was afflicted with some unspecified disease to remind him that a sense of one's own superiority in any respect is a denial of God's grace and so a disqualification for doing God's work.

Gospel   Mark 6: 1–6

This passage is in marked contrast with last Sunday's Gospel which immediately precedes it in Mark, but it further emphasizes the point that faith in Jesus is an essential condition for receiving the gift of life which he offers. The incident itself would be a commonplace one if it were not for the identity of the central figure, which is concealed from the other participants but known to the reader. These people have rejected the words and signs of life unwittingly, but not therefore excusably; their inability to accept the possibility of God's activity in familiar, ordinary things is a fundamental lack of faith which disqualifies them from receiving the gift of life.

Fifteenth Sunday in Ordinary Time

God has chosen and called us to holiness and to the inheritance of his promises.

First Reading   **Amos 7: 12–15**

Amos was called away from his farm in the southern kingdom of Judah to proclaim God's word to the people of the northern kingdom of Israel. But at the royal sanctuary of Bethel he encountered the hostility of the priest Amaziah, who drove him away. Amaziah's contemptuous dismissal of Amos as a charlatan who prophesied simply to earn his keep ('bread') led him to 'present his credentials'. In line with other great prophets of the Old Testament (e.g. Isaiah, Jeremiah, Ezekiel) he asserted that his prophetic mission was undertaken not of his own volition but in answer to a specific call from God which could not be denied.

Responsorial Psalm   **85 (84)**

℟ *Let us see, O Lord, your mercy*
  and give us your saving help.

1 I will hear what the Lord God has to say,
   a voice that speaks of peace,
   peace for his people.
   His help is near for those who fear him
   and his glory will dwell in our land. (R)

2 Mercy and faithfulness have met;
   justice and peace have embraced.
   Faithfulness shall spring from the earth
   and justice look down from heaven. (R)

3 The Lord will make us prosper
   and our earth shall yield its fruit.
   Justice shall march before him
   and peace shall follow his steps. (R)

This Psalm begins as a communal lament (see p. 12); but this final section is an expression of confidence in which the worshippers' dejection is overcome by meditation on the nature of God as one who loves his people and will surely restore his blessing and salvation to them.

Second Reading   Ephesians 1: 3–14

This passage, the opening section of the Epistle to the Ephesians, is a great hymn of praise to God the Father which sets out in closely packed phrases the whole of the work of Christ for his people. Salvation is presented in cosmic terms and in the perspective of eternity, stretching from the election of the faithful from before the foundation of the world to the consummation of all things when they will enter into the fulness of their inheritance. The themes of God's call to holiness and of the proclamation of the word of God which characterize the Old Testament reading are here taken up again in connection with the theme of God's plan of salvation: the fact that we were chosen from before the foundation of the world emphasizes the divine initiative, the call which cannot be denied; and the means by which that call was communicated to us was the word of truth, the gospel of our salvation. It is important to notice that the hymn has a Trinitarian shape: God the Father destined us to be his sons through Jesus Christ who has redeemed us, and the Holy Spirit is the guarantor of the fruits of this redemption.

Gospel   Mark 6: 7–13

Jesus' ministry of preaching and teaching (6: 6) and of healing (5: 35–43) is here extended: Jesus now sends out the Twelve, whom he has previously appointed (3: 13–19), to share in the tasks which they have now seen him perform. He gives them 'authority', that is, his effective power, sufficient for these tasks. The instructions which he gives them before they set out may reflect the practice of the early Christian missionaries. The message with which the Twelve are charged, the call to repent because the kingdom of God is at hand, is identical with that of Jesus himself (1: 15). There are, however, some significant differences in the other actions of the Twelve and those performed by Jesus himself: there is no mention of their raising the dead to life (cf. 5: 35–43); and the healing of the sick is carried out by the instrumentality of oil, which Jesus never used for this purpose. The use of oil again probably reflects later Christian practice; but the passage as a whole stresses the fact that the actions performed by disciples in Jesus' name are on the one hand limited in scope compared with his, but on the other hand performed with fulness of his own power, delegated to them.

Sixteenth Sunday in Ordinary Time

Jesus Christ is the Good Shepherd who gathers and protects his flock.

First Reading   Jeremiah 23: 1–6

The Old Testament frequently uses the term 'shepherd' in a sense common among the peoples of the ancient Near East which surrounded Israel: that of ruler or king. God is the chief shepherd of his chosen people Israel, and its kings are appointed by him to rule on his behalf. In this passage, however, the prophet, speaking in God's name, condemns the contemporary rulers of Judah for pursuing policies contrary to his will which have already resulted in the scattering of part of the nation through deportation to Babylon. But he also promises to restore to these exiles both their homes and their prosperity, and to make a new beginning by appointing new 'shepherds' who will protect the newly gathered 'flock' and care for it. The last part of the passage, probably originally independent of the first, identifies these promised 'shepherds': they will be the descendants of David, the old Davidic dynasty restored. This idealized picture of future blessedness was never to be realized within the history of old Israel, but the Christian Church has seen it as a prophecy of the Messiah.

Responsorial Psalm 23 (22)

℞ *The Lord is my shepherd;*
there is nothing I shall want.

1 The Lord is my shepherd;
there is nothing I shall want.
Fresh and green are the pastures
where he gives me repose.
Near restful waters he leads me,
to revive my drooping spirit. (R)

2 He guides me along the right path;
he is true to his name.
If I should walk in the valley of darkness
no evil would I fear.
You are there with your crook and your staff;
with these you give me comfort. (R)

3 You have prepared a banquet for me
in the sight of my foes.
My head you have anointed with oil;
my cup is overflowing. (R)

4 Surely goodness and kindness shall follow me
all the days of my life.
In the Lord's own house shall I dwell
for ever and ever. (R)

In this Psalm, perhaps best described as a Psalm of confidence (see p. 12) the thought of God as shepherd is individualized. The worshipper expresses his confidence in God as the one who can be relied upon to provide all his needs and to guide and protect him all his life.

Second Reading **Ephesians 2: 13–18**

In several passages in the New Testament, of which the parable of the Good Shepherd in John 10 is the most familiar, the term 'shepherd' is applied to Jesus as the one who completely fulfils the role of shepherd of God's flock pictured in the Old Testament. In this passage the word is not used, but the full implications of the role of Christ as the shepherd are drawn out. The 'flock' is now understood as enormously extended in scope: it is no longer restricted to the Jews or Israelites. The epistle is addressed to non-Jewish Christians, and the main point of the passage is that through the redemptive work of Christ on the Cross all those men and women who were once outside the 'flock' as conceived in the Old Testament but who have responded to the preaching of the gospel have been brought within the fold: Christ himself is the 'peace', that is, the creator of a new single redeemed humanity. As in John 10, where the Good Shepherd gives his life for the flock, this has been made possible only by the sacrifice of Christ on the Cross.

Gospel   **Mark 6: 30–34**

This passage is the sequel to the story of the sending out of the twelve apostles (see last week's Gospel). The apostles return from their mission and make their report to Jesus. Jesus then takes them away from the crowds to a lonely place to rest after their exertions. This is an example and pattern of the Christian life, in which the active work of preaching and witnessing to the gospel is only made possible and effective if periods are set aside for both physical and spiritual rest and refreshment. In the ministry of Jesus and his disciples such periods were and are, however, often very brief: the needs of the world continually press upon them. Here again the shepherd theme appears: men and women without Jesus Christ are like sheep without a shepherd; and Jesus, moved as always by love and pity, begins again to give them the teaching which they need and for which they have come to him.

Seventeenth Sunday in Ordinary Time

Christ supplies all our needs, both physical and spiritual.

First Reading   **2 Kings 4: 42–44**

This is one of a series of miracle-stories attributed to the prophet Elisha. Several of them recount miracles which he is said to have performed for the benefit of members of certain groups of prophets known as the 'sons of the prophets', which were a feature of Israelite

life in the ninth century BC, the century before that of the so-called
'classical' prophets Hosea, Amos and Isaiah. Elisha, though he
frequently acted quite independently of these groups, had a special
connection with them, and these stories were at first probably
handed down in their circles. This story, like some of the others,
ought probably to be regarded as pious legend rather than as history.
It reflects the impression which Elisha made on those who knew him
best and who clearly believed that he could do anything. We should
note, however, that this is not a hero-story, nor is Elisha regarded as
a magician possessing miraculous powers of his own. He acts only in
accordance with the word of God, who is the source of life and of the
life-giving fruits of the earth. The story anticipates the accounts in
the Gospels of the feeding of the multitudes by Jesus.

Responsorial Psalm 145 (144)

℟ *You open wide your hand, O Lord,*
and grant our desires.

1 All your creatures shall thank you, O Lord,
   and your friends shall repeat their blessing.
   They shall speak of the glory of your reign
   and declare your might, O God. (R)

2 The eyes of all creatures look to you
   and you give them their food in due time.
   You open wide your hand,
   grant the desires of all who live. (R)

3 The Lord is just in all his ways
   and loving in all his deeds.
   He is close to all who call him,
   who call on him from their hearts. (R)

This Psalm is a song of thanksgiving (see p. 12) which praises God
for many gifts, including his gift of life-giving food.

Second Reading **Ephesians 4: 1–6**

Earlier in this epistle the apostle wrote of the Christian calling and of
our participation in the fruits of the redemptive work of Christ. Now
he writes in more detail of the quality of the Christian life. He

returns to the theme expounded in last week's Epistle of the oneness of the new humanity which Christ created by his death on the Cross. This 'unity of the Spirit' is a gift already given to the Church, but if it is to be maintained and realized to the full, each member must show himself worthy of it by practising those virtues which make for peace and harmony: selflessness, gentleness, patience. The Church in New Testament times was no more exempt from divisive and self-seeking tendencies than it is today, as many passages, especially in St. Paul's epistles, show us. This passage ends with a massive exposition of the essential unity of the Church and its dependence on the unity of God – the word 'one' occurs no less than seven times in the last few phrases. This is a rhetorical *tour de force* in a sense, not intended to be an attack on specific divisions within the Church; but it should nevertheless stir the modern Christian to reflect how far the Church today is failing to measure up to the vision here presented to us.

Gospel   John 6: 1–15

In each of the four Gospels there is an account of the miraculous feeding of five thousand people by Jesus; and the theme itself, as this week's Old Testament reading shows, had a long ancestry. Each of the four accounts has its own characteristics, but that of John, as in the case of some other miracles, is the most distinctive. It is one of a series of 'signs' (the word has this special meaning for John) each of which is narrated in a way intended to bring out vividly a particular aspect of our Lord's nature and work. To understand what the incident meant for John it is necessary to read the remainder of this chapter, which is a kind of meditation on it. This later part of the chapter contains Jesus' words 'I am the bread of life. He who comes to me will never be hungry; he who believes in me will never thirst'. These words are the true key to the story as John tells it. Jesus is himself the gift from God which brings not merely physical but eternal life to men and women.

Eighteenth Sunday in Ordinary Time

Christ is the true bread from heaven who gives us eternal life.

First Reading   **Exodus 16: 2–4, 12–15**

It is to this incident that the people refer in today's Gospel when they speak about the 'bread from heaven' which their ancestors had eaten in the desert. This passage from the book of Exodus speaks of God's love and care for his people who were, or claimed to be, in danger of starvation in the desert. The miraculous element in the story lies not in the food provided, for which there are natural explanations, but in its provision at the very moment when it was needed and in the sufficiency of the quantity provided. But the writer is concerned to stress not simply the love and grace of God shown in yet another chapter in Israel's history, but the circumstances in which the gifts were given. The accounts in the books of Exodus and Numbers of the journey of the Israelites through the desert after their flight from Egypt on their way to the Promised Land are punctuated with stories of this kind in which the people display an entire lack of trust in God and in his servant Moses whom he has appointed to lead them, voicing bitter complaints about their hardships and dangers. Their only concern, as with the crowds in today's Gospel, is with the immediate satisfaction of their bodily needs.

Responsorial Psalm   **78 (77)**

℟ *The Lord gave them bread from heaven.*

1 The things we have heard and understood,
   the things our fathers have told us,
   we will tell to the next generation:
   the glories of the Lord and his might. (R)

2 He commanded the clouds above
   and opened the gates of heaven.
   He rained down manna for their food,
   and gave them bread from heaven. (R)

3 Mere men ate the bread of angels.
   He sent them abundance of food.
   He brought them to his holy land,
   to the mountain which his right hand had won. (R)

This is a short extract from a very long Psalm, one of the so-called 'historical Psalms', which retells the story of God's love and care for his people from early times to the time of David. These verses include a reference to the incident recounted in today's Old Testament reading.

Second Reading   **Ephesians 4: 17, 20–24**

The apostle here further develops the theme which he introduced in last Sunday's Epistle. His readers, who have only recently been converted to the Christian faith, are told that their Christian profession must be accompanied by a complete change in their way of life. The life led by the non-Christians among whom they live and work is described as the aimless pursuit of worthless and unworthy desires. To become a Christian is to undergo a complete spiritual revolution: the abandonment of the old self and the assumption of a new. This new self is the creation of God, and is characterized by goodness and holiness. This exhortation is of course relevant not only to new converts but equally to all Christians who live, as in our own day, in a largely pagan environment; Christians must always be aware that they belong first not to the world but to Christ, and must frame their conduct in accordance with the truth which they have found in him.

Gospel   **John 6: 24–35**

After the feeding of the five thousand narrated in last Sunday's Gospel, Jesus withdrew once more with his disciples from the crowds, crossing the sea by boat and landing on the other side at Capernaum. But many of the crowd followed him. Jesus, however, knew that they had followed him not because of his teaching but because they saw him as one who could fill their bellies. If they made him their national leader, as we are told at the end of last Sunday's Gospel they wanted to do, they would be able to live a life of ease, with their material needs miraculously provided for. In the conversation which follows, Jesus sought to use this gross misunderstanding of his mission as an opportunity to show them what were their real spiritual needs, and how he, as the spiritual 'food' sent by his

Father like the manna in the desert, could give them the only true satisfaction, which is eternal life.

Nineteenth Sunday in Ordinary Time

Christ is the true bread from heaven who gives us eternal life.

First Reading   **1 Kings 19: 4–8**

This story about Elijah has no doubt been chosen as the Old Testament reading because of its reference to miraculously provided food in the desert, a theme which runs through most of the readings set for recent Sundays. Elijah, the fearless prophet of the Lord, has been forced by his arch-enemy Jezebel, queen of Israel and wife of king Ahab, to flee into the desert. It seems to him that he has failed in his attempt to stem the progress of paganism in Israel which Jezebel is assiduously fostering. Like Moses, who also had been Israel's spiritual leader and who also sometimes came close to despair, Elijah makes a journey through the desert under the guidance of God, is miraculously fed there, and is drawn towards the mountain of God (known sometimes as Horeb, sometimes as Sinai) where he is to have a decisive personal encounter with God himself. Like the quails and the manna provided for the people of Israel (see the Old Testament reading for last Sunday) food is given him for the journey. On Elijah's journey, the sinful people are left behind; but after his encounter with God Elijah will return to them with strength renewed to resume his struggle to defend the true faith.

Responsorial Psalm   34 (33)

℞ *Taste and see that the Lord is good.*

1 I will bless the Lord at all times,
    his praise always on my lips;
    in the Lord my soul shall make its boast.
    The humble shall hear and be glad. (R)

2 Glorify the Lord with me.
    Together let us praise his name.

I sought the Lord and he answered me;
from all my terrors he set me free. (R)

3 Look towards him and be radiant;
let your faces not be abashed.
This poor man called; the Lord heard him
and rescued him from all his distress. (R)

4 The angel of the Lord is encamped
around those who revere him, to rescue them.
Taste and see that the Lord is good.
He is happy who seeks refuge in him. (R)

A song of thanksgiving (see p. 12) which is mainly in the form of an exhortation to others to thank God for his goodness and for his protection of his faithful ones.

Second Reading   **Ephesians 4: 30–5: 2**

Continuing his exhortation to his readers to change their way of life in accordance with their newly acquired faith, the apostle becomes more specific, listing certain characteristics of the pagan way of life which they must now shun and certain virtues which are characteristic of and essential to the Christian way of life. The vices and virtues which he lists are all concerned with human relationships: the life of pagans is characterized by selfishness and enmity as each person tries to obtain an advantage over others. Such behaviour is the antithesis of a true society. The Christian life, on the other hand, is characterized by mutual support and love for others, building up the body of Christ which is the only true society. The way to acquire the Christian virtues is by the imitation of God as he is revealed in the earthly life of Christ: a life of love, forgiveness, and total self-sacrifice. Such conduct in the Christian is pleasing to the Holy Spirit, of whose abiding presence with us our baptism is the seal and guarantee.

Gospel   **John 6: 41–51**

Jesus' claim to be the bread of life raises the crucial question of his status and of his relationship to the Father. The Jews ask how one who is clearly a man like themselves can at the same time have come down from heaven, that is, from God. In this passage Jesus does not answer this question directly; rather he asserts more explicitly and more uncompromisingly than before his claim to uniqueness. He has indeed been sent by the Father to be the only means by which men and women can have access to him. Eternal life can only be obtained through belief in him. Finally he makes an even more shocking statement: his being the bread, or food, from heaven means that he will give his own flesh as food for the life of the world. The Christian reader would see here a reference both to the Cross and to the Eucharist; but to the Jews who heard these words the statement would have been both incomprehensible and deeply offensive. Christian belief is here deliberately presented as forcing men and women to make a critical decision: it is totally unacceptable to the world and can only be acceptable to those whose faith in Jesus is absolute. To the latter it is the way to eternal life.

Twentieth Sunday in Ordinary Time

Christ is the true bread from heaven who gives us eternal life.

First Reading   **Proverbs 9: 1–6**

In part of the book of Proverbs and in Ecclesiasticus and the Wisdom of Solomon, 'wisdom' is personified: it is represented as a living person, a woman. Here she builds a seven-pillared house and then issues a general invitation to a house-warming party. In this short poem no direct indication is given of her identity, and in the poem itself, before it was placed in its present context, it was not implied that wisdom has any special relationship with God. But in its present context in the book of Proverbs wisdom is understood to be God's own Wisdom, with which he created and maintains the world and which he grants to men and women who seek him. The feast to which Wisdom invites the simple and ignorant thus becomes a symbol of the knowledge of God and of his ways which is freely available to those who sincerely wish to have it. The strange personification of Wisdom and the meaning of some of the symbolism, especially of the house and its seven pillars, are not completely understood, but the editor of the book may have possessed some insight into the nature of God which to some extent anticipated the differentiation of a plurality of Persons in the one Godhead which is expressed in the doctrine of the Holy Trinity. In 1 Corinthians 1: 24 and elsewhere in the New Testament the Wisdom of God is identified with Christ.

Responsorial Psalm   34 (33)

℟ *Taste and see that the Lord is good.*

1 I will bless the Lord at all times,
    his praise always on my lips;
    in the Lord my soul shall make its boast.
    The humble shall hear and be glad. (R)

2 Revere the Lord, you his saints.
    They lack nothing, those who revere him.
    Strong lions suffer want and go hungry
    but those who seek the Lord lack no blessing. (R)

3 Come, children, and hear me
    that I may teach you the fear of the Lord.
    Who is he who longs for life
    and many days, to enjoy his prosperity? (R)

4 Then keep your tongue from evil
    and your lips from speaking deceit.
    Turn aside from evil and do good;
    seek and strive after peace. (R)

In these verses, which form part of a Psalm of thanksgiving, the speaker invites his audience to worship God for his goodness and to behave in such a way as to deserve his blessings.

Second Reading   **Ephesians 5: 15–20**

Here the apostle exhorts his readers to show wisdom in the way in which they live their lives as Christians. In a world that is evil they are to use this God-given wisdom to ascertain what is God's will and to apply this knowledge responsibly in their daily actions. He draws a contrast between drunkenness – being filled with wine – which is characteristic of the folly of the pagan world, and being filled instead with the Holy Spirit, a state which will express itself in a peculiarly Christian kind of self-abandonment, namely breaking out into songs of a spiritual rather than an intoxicated kind. The criterion of this spiritual light-heartedness is that what is done is done in the name of Christ and in a spirit of thankfulness to God.

Gospel   **John 6: 51–58**

The miracle which Jesus has performed in feeding the five thousand has attracted a crowd which has come to him for the wrong reason: they think that he will use his miraculous powers to make life easy for them. Jesus here draws a contrast between the bread which he gave them to satisfy their immediate physical needs and the true 'living bread' which will permanently satisfy their spiritual needs, giving them eternal life. But when he claims that he himself is this living bread, and goes on to make the even more astonishing statement that eternal life can only be obtained by eating his flesh and drinking his blood, the Jews are, not surprisingly, deeply shocked and think that he is mad. For the Christian reader, however, this is an unmistakable reference to the Eucharist. Like the other discourses of Jesus in John, this discourse is addressed to a Christian audience though put in the form of an address to the Jews. The extraordinary claims made by Jesus about himself are thus represented as a cause of Jesus' rejection by the vast majority of the Jewish people.

Twenty-first Sunday in Ordinary Time

Divine grace takes the initiative, but demands a response of commitment and obedience.

First Reading   **Joshua 24: 1–2, 15–18**

After Joshua had led the people of Israel across the Jordan into the Promised Land, he conquered the land and subdued its inhabitants, dividing it up between the tribes. Such is the sequence of events which followed the death of Moses as presented to us by the editor of the book of Joshua. Whether his account of the events is reliable or not is not our concern now. More important are the religious lessons which the editor wished to teach his readers. Much of this teaching is summarized in the final chapter of the book, of which a short extract is given in this Old Testament reading, and which narrates Joshua's last action before his death. In his speech to the tribes gathered at Shechem he reminded them how their ancestors had been pagans worshipping other gods until the Lord had intervened and chosen Abraham, who is not said to have been any less pagan than his contemporaries or to have deserved any special favour, and taken him away from his pagan environment, showering blessings both on him and on his descendants, later leading them out of slavery in Egypt and finally giving them the land in which they are now living. All this the Lord did for his people out of pure grace. But now they must come to a decision: they must serve him alone, or serve other gods. There can be no compromise.

Responsorial Psalm   34 (33)

℞ *Taste and see that the Lord is good.*

1 I will bless the Lord at all times,
    his praise always on my lips;
    in the Lord my soul shall make its boast.
    The humble shall hear and be glad. (R)

2 The Lord turns his face against the wicked
    to destroy their remembrance from the earth.
    The Lord turns his eyes to the just
    and his ears to their appeal. (R)

3 They call and the Lord hears
    and rescues them in all their distress.
    The Lord is close to the broken-hearted;
    those whose spirit is crushed he will save. (R)

4 Many are the trials of the just man
    but from them all the Lord will rescue him.
    He will keep guard over all his bones,
    not one of his bones shall be broken. (R)

5 Evil brings death to the wicked;
    those who hate the good are doomed.
    The Lord ransoms the souls of his servants.
    Those who hide in him shall not be condemned. (R)

Another section of the Psalm. In these verses the speaker exhorts his audience to praise God especially for his protection of the 'just man' when he is attacked by enemies. 'Just man' in the Psalms often means 'religious' or 'faithful to God' rather than 'righteous'.

Second Reading   **Ephesians 5: 21–32**

As with several other of the New Testament epistles, the last part of the epistle to the Ephesians is devoted to detailed instructions about the way in which Christians should live their lives. This passage is concerned with the relationship which ought to exist between husbands and wives. The apostle takes for granted the universal view of his time that wives ought to be subject to their husbands. The fact that this is no longer acceptable to us does not mean that this passage can be dismissed as simply outmoded. More important than the idea of male pre-eminence, which belonged to the age in which the epistle was written, is the principle of mutual respect with which the passage begins. Equally important is the principle of marital love, which is to be like that of Christ for his Church, self-sacrificing and deeply caring.

Gospel   **John 6: 60–69**

That part of Jesus' teaching which some of his followers are here said to have found intolerable is his claim, made just before, that he is the bread which came down from heaven and that only by eating his flesh and drinking his blood can eternal life be obtained. Like the tribes of Israel in today's Old Testament reading, those who have followed Jesus so far are abruptly brought to the point of decision: they must accept totally the claims which he makes for himself or they must leave him and cease to be his disciples. Some of them choose the latter course. Jesus comments on this reaction that discipleship is a mystery which depends on the inscrutable will of God. The Twelve, however, with Simon Peter as their spokesman, decide the other way. They recognize that nowhere else is the message of eternal life to be found, and they have also come to recognize Jesus' unique relationship to the Father. In making their decision they commit themselves totally to him.

Twenty-second Sunday in Ordinary Time

True religion expresses itself in obedience to the moral law.

First Reading   **Deuteronomy 4: 1–2, 6–8**

In the book of Deuteronomy Moses is represented as giving a final address to the people of Israel in the land of Moab on the brink of the Promised Land, which they are to enter after his death by crossing the Jordan. The greater part of the book consists of the report of this address, in which Moses reminds the people of what God has done for them in the past and warns them that if they are to succeed in conquering the land and prospering in it they must obey God's laws, which he then expounds to them in great detail. To keep God's laws, however, should not be regarded as a burden but as a privilege which has been granted to no other people.

Responsorial Psalm   **15 (14)**

℟ *Lord, who shall be admitted to your tent?*

1 Lord, who shall dwell on your holy mountain?
    He who walks without fault;
    he who acts with justice
    and speaks the truth from his heart. (R)

2 He who does no wrong to his brother,
    who casts no slur on his neighbour,
    who holds the godless in disdain,
    but honours those who fear the Lord. (R)

3 He who keeps his pledge, come what may;
    who takes no interest on a loan
    and accepts no bribes against the innocent.
    Such a man will stand firm for ever. (R)

This Psalm lists the characteristics required of those who come to worship at God's Temple. It may originally have been used as part of the preparations required of pilgrims before they were permitted to enter the Temple precincts.

Second Reading   James 1: 17–18, 21–22, 27

The little epistle of James emphasizes the importance for the Christian of a high standard of moral conduct. In this passage the author begins by reminding his readers that their status as children of God is derived entirely from God's creative and unchangeable word, the message of the gospel, and that they are intended to be a kind of model or example of God's full plan for the salvation of all mankind. But they are not yet perfect, and must strive to become pure and worthy of their new status. To help them to do this God has provided them with the word of the gospel, which he has actually planted within them, in their consciences. Even with this help it is only too easy to deceive oneself about one's conduct. Obedience to God's will requires close and constant attention to it. Unless our religion expresses itself in terms of such things as generosity to those in need and avoidance of the corrupt standards of the world, it will not be regarded by God as true religion at all.

Gospel   Mark 7: 1–8, 14–15, 21–23

One of the matters on which Jesus came into conflict with the Pharisees was that they had elaborated a system of rules and regulations for daily life which had no authority in Scripture, and which they sought to impose on others, while they neglected God's real commandments. The specific question at issue here is the Pharisaic regulations concerning purity, which required the frequent washing of cups and dishes as well as of hands before meals – not from ordinary motives of cleanliness, but in order to avoid supposed spiritual contamination from contact with people regarded as spiritually unclean. Jesus was questioned about his refusal to observe these customs, and took the opportunity to teach the ordinary people about the real nature of purity and defilement. Sin or impurity arises from within a person, from his inner being. This is not an attack on all religious observances, many of which Jesus himself practised, but rather puts them in their proper place. No amount of religious observance in itself can be of any avail while we still nurture in our hearts sinful desires, whether or not these express themselves in actual sinful acts.

Twenty-third Sunday in Ordinary Time

First Reading   Isaiah 35: 4–7

This chapter speaks of a miraculous transformation of a desert into a fruitful land. Since it ends with a prophecy that a sacred highway will be built across it along which God's redeemed ones will pass joyfully, it seems originally to have foretold, like some passages in Isaiah 40–55, the triumphant return to their homeland of the Jews exiled in Babylonia in the sixth century BC. Many of the details of the description, however, are derived from more general beliefs held in Israel about God's redemptive and miraculous activity which seemed to the author appropriate to such a moment in history. As a result of passages such as this, God's healing activity manifested in other Old Testament passages – giving sight to the blind, hearing to the deaf and so on – led to a belief among the Jews in the period preceding the birth of Christ that such activity would be signs of the arrival of the messianic age; and this belief is reflected in the accounts of Jesus' healing miracles such as that described in today's Gospel. This belief is also reflected in the incident when John the Baptist sent his disciples to enquire of Jesus whether he was the Messiah. The only answer which Jesus gave was to refer to the fact that such healing miracles were being performed (Matthew 11: 4–5; Luke 7: 22).

Responsorial Psalm   146 (145)

℟ *My soul, gives praise to the Lord.*
  or *Alleluia!*

1 It is the Lord who keeps faith for ever,
  who is just to those who are oppressed.
  It is he who gives bread to the hungry,
  the Lord, who sets prisoners free. (R)

2 It is the Lord who gives sight to the blind,
  who raises up those who are bowed down,
  the Lord who loves the just,
  the Lord, who protects the stranger. (R)

3 The Lord upholds the widow and orphan,
but thwarts the path of the wicked.
The Lord will reign for ever,
Zion's God, from age to age. Alleluia! (R)

A hymn of praise (see p. 12). In these verses God is especially praised for the help and protection which he gives to the oppressed and the unfortunate.

Second Reading   **James 2: 1–5**

This passage speaks for itself. It is astonishing and sobering to learn from it that even in the earliest days of the Church some members had already so far forgotten or corrupted the teaching of Jesus as to endanger the principle of the unity of all believers in Christ by introducing class distinctions and favoured treatment of the rich into their assemblies. The author of the epistle, however, condemns such practices not so much on the grounds of the unity of all Christians as on those of the much more revolutionary doctrine, found in the teaching of Jesus (for example in the parable of the rich man and Lazarus) and also in some parts of the Old Testament – that God overturns human categories and especially loves the poor, who have a prior claim over the rich to be heirs of his kingdom.

Gospel   **Mark 7: 31–37**

Jesus' reputation as a healer had preceded him, and even when he made a journey through foreign territory the people were eager for his help. The details given here of the means by which he healed the deaf and dumb man are unique. There were other itinerant healers in the pagan world at that time, and such methods may have been used by them. The evangelist may have included these details to show that Jesus did not despise any method of healing.

The fact that Jesus tried to prevent the witnesses from spreading the news of the miracle shows that it was not his intention to acquire a reputation as a wonder-worker, or to win acclamation by the Jews as the Messiah (see the notes on today's Old Testament reading). This is an important point. The truth of the gospel does not and cannot rest on the fact that Jesus performed miracles. The miracles were rather the natural consequence of his divine nature coupled with his compassion for those who were sick. The miracle-stories do not have the character of proof-texts and would not be accepted as such by non-believers. The defence of the truth of Christianity must be undertaken on other grounds.

Twenty-fourth Sunday in Ordinary Time

First Reading   Isaiah 50: 5–9

This is the third of the passages in Isaiah known as the Suffering Servant Songs, because they depict one who accepts unjust suffering from men as part of his service of God. The writer may originally have been referring to Israel in its sufferings under other nations, or some idealized representative of Israel. These passages seem to have inspired Jesus with the idea of a Messiah who suffered, and so enabled him to do his work for mankind. Christians interpret the songs as referring to him, since he fills the part perfectly. This song emphasizes the Servant's readiness to accept suffering and his trust that God will vindicate him in the end.

Responsorial Psalm   116 (114)

℟ *I will walk in the presence of the Lord*
   in the land of the living.
   or *Alleluia!*

1 Alleluia!
   I love the Lord for he has heard
   the cry of my appeal;
   for he turned his ear to me
   in the day when I called him. (R)

2 They surrounded me, the snares of death,
   with the anguish of the tomb;
   they caught me, sorrow and distress.
   I called on the Lord's name.
   O Lord my God, deliver me! (R)

3 How gracious is the Lord, and just;
   our God has compassion.

The Lord protects the simple hearts;
I was helpless so he saved me. (R)

4 He has kept my soul from death,
my eyes from tears
and my feet from stumbling.
I will walk in the presence of the Lord
in the land of the living. (R)

In this hymn of thanksgiving for deliverance, the psalmist repeats
the themes of Isaiah: he was beset by suffering and death, but the
Lord answered his cry for help.

Second Reading   **James 2: 14–18**

James emphasizes practical religion. He may be reacting to a perver-
sion of Paul's doctrine that our fellowship with God depends not on
our good deeds (see Gal. 3), but on our faith in Christ. This could be
distorted so as to suggest that good deeds do not matter at all – a very
different point. James therefore supposes a man who claims to have
faith, but shows no care for his fellow men: he needs the opposite
treatment from Paul's readers, because his lack of love shows that he
really has no faith in the first place. Paul was dealing with men who
thought their good deeds put God in their debt; James with men
who thought that right beliefs were all that mattered, whether or not
they loved others.

Gospel   **Mark 8: 27–35**

Here, for the first time in Mark's Gospel, Jesus is solemnly recognized as the Messiah by Peter, who may have been the only one to see
it, or may have been voicing the thoughts of the other disciples.
'Messiah' (in Greek, 'Christ') means 'anointed': the one whom, in
Jesus' time, many of the Jews expected God to send to liberate them
from Rome and restore their independent kingdom.

Jesus' next words then come as a shock. Peter had acclaimed him
as the Messiah, but instead of military conquest he will suffer death,
and only then be saved by the intervention of God. Peter has the
usual idea about the Messiah; he has seen truly who Jesus is, but now

how Jesus will do the Messiah's work. That will be through suffering, and the same path lies ahead for his followers.

Twenty-fifth Sunday in Ordinary Time

First Reading   **Wisdom 2: 12, 17–20**

In this reading the tormenting of the innocent is presented from the side of his persecutors, instead of (as last week) from his. They hate the virtuous man because he exposes their wickedness: they will torment him and see if his virtue will stand up to it. If he is 'God's son' – Hebrew idiom for a godly man – God will look after him.

Christians of course see Christ's sufferings foreshadowed here. His perfection aroused the wicked to have him killed; in some sense it was the wickedness of all mankind that tested his goodness to the breaking point of death; and God did look after him. We also take 'God's son' in a way the writer would not have dreamed of.

Responsorial Psalm   54 (53)

℟ *The Lord upholds my life.*

1 O God, save me by your name;
    by your power, uphold my cause.
    O God, hear my prayer;
    listen to the words of my mouth. (R)

2 For proud men have risen against me,
    ruthless men seek my life.
    They have no regard for God. (R)

3 But I have God for my help.
    The Lord upholds my life.
    I will sacrifice to you with willing heart
    and praise your name for it is good. (R)

A Psalm of individual lament (cf. p. 12) in which the psalmist puts his trust in God. Such is his confidence that he considers his liberation already achieved.

Second Reading   **James 3: 16–4: 3**

James contemplates the enmities between men. First he contrasts them with the heavenly wisdom from above, which spreads love and peace. Peacemakers do its work when they bring enemies together, and their work bears lasting fruit.

Secondly, he sees that disharmony between men springs from the disharmony within them. The inward faults of those obstinately set on getting their own way will inevitably bring them into conflict with others. Even their prayers are infected by their selfishness, so that they feel resentment when their prayers are not answered.

This reading relates to the others: for the good man who suffers is an embodiment of the heavenly wisdom which makes for peace, and Jesus is the perfect example.

Gospel   **Mark 9: 30–37**

The first part is the second prediction by Jesus, recorded in Mark, of his coming suffering and resurrection (the first was in last Sunday's Gospel). The disciples are unable to grasp it; they still expect Jesus to bring in God's kingdom by a spectacular act, and their ideas about greatness are on the same worldly level.

He has heard them discussing their own relative greatness (perhaps of the positions they will hold in the Kingdom) and sees that they have not yet learned the lesson of renunciation. He puts it in a new way: anyone wanting to be first must be last of all. God works through men's self-forgetfulness, not their assertiveness. Their concern should be with humility, like that of the little child; then they will do things in Jesus' way, which is the way of God.

Twenty-sixth Sunday in Ordinary Time

Goodness is not confined to ourselves, nor evil to others.

First Reading   **Numbers 11: 25–29**

This scene takes place in the desert after the Israelites have left Sinai. They have a portable sanctuary, the Tent, which they pitch in a separate place outside their camp whenever they halt on the journey. The Cloud of God's presence hovers over the Tent, and he communicates with Moses there.

The 'spirit' is here thought of as God's power enabling a man to prophesy – to speak under his direct influence. On this occasion Moses is not the only one inspired; so are the elders of Israel who have been standing round the Tent, though they prophesy only for a time. Even two of the elders who stayed at a distance, in the camp, are similarly inspired. This scandalizes Joshua, who is jealous for Moses' supremacy; but Moses himself wishes all to have the same inspiration as himself.

Responsorial Psalm   **19 (18)**

℞ *The precepts of the Lord gladden the heart.*

1 The law of the Lord is perfect,
   it revives the soul.
   The rule of the Lord is to be trusted,
   it gives wisdom to the simple. (R)

2 The fear of the Lord is holy,
   abiding for ever.
   The decrees of the Lord are truth
   and all of them just. (R)

3 So in them your servant finds instruction;
   great reward is in their keeping.
   But who can detect all his errors?
   From hidden faults acquit me. (R)

4 From presumption restrain your servant
   and let it not rule me.
   Then shall I be blameless,
   clean from grave sin. (R)

The Psalm praises God whose inspiration is available to guide men and keep them from sin. The sentiments reflect the law-piety of post-exilic Judaism.

Second Reading   James 5: 1-6

There is an ambiguous attitude to wealth in the Bible. It is rejoiced in as a gift – perhaps even a reward – from God, especially in the Old Testament, though the rich man is expected to be generous and charitable to others. In practice the rich too often enjoy their luxury and neglect or oppress the poor, and this theme is to be found in the prophets, Jesus, and here in James. He accuses the rich of positive injustice, even of murder; but God is aware of all, and in the end they will get their due punishment.

Gospel   Mark 9: 38-43, 45, 47-48

The first section resumes the theme of the first reading. Jesus has the Spirit, and not only speaks but exorcizes in God's power; to some extent the disciples do so too. John, like Joshua, is offended because an 'outsider' has acted in God's name just as if he were one of Jesus' known disciples. Jesus' reaction is like Moses': God's power is not confined to the 'official channels', and any who show they are acting in God's power are doing the same work and must be welcomed.

The second section turns the question on its head: what about the 'insiders' who, for all their official status, sin as badly as the rest? They deserve judgement as much as the proverbially wicked denounced by James; even more, they must actively judge them-selves, discern the particular things that lead them to sin, and eradicate them as ruthlessly as if cutting off a limb (an example of Jesus' extreme use of language about the deepest things in religion and life).

Twenty-seventh Sunday in Ordinary Time

God wants mankind to be a unity, and the human family is this unity in microcosm.

First Reading   Genesis 2: 18–24

This is the climax of the second Creation story: less grand and cosmic than the first one in Genesis 1, and more anthropomorphic. All the subhuman creatures have been named by man (a sign of his power over them). None can give him companionship and help on his own level. So God makes him a fit companion out of part of himself: that is, she is of his own kind, as his first words recognize. The story signifies the unity, difference, and mutual fitness of man and woman, and the writer explains that this is the basis of marriage, where the unity can be expressed by such a strong term as 'one body'.

Responsorial Psalm   128 (127)

℞ *May the Lord bless us*
  all the days of our life.

1 O blessed are those who fear the Lord
   and walk in his ways!
   By the labour of your hands you shall eat.
   You will be happy and prosper. (R)

2 Your wife will be like a fruitful vine
   in the heart of your house;
   your children like shoots of the olive,
   around your table. (R)

3 Indeed thus shall be blessed
   the man who fears the Lord.
   May the Lord bless you from Zion
   in a happy Jerusalem
   all the days of your life!
   May you see your children's children.
   On Israel, peace! (R)

This Wisdom Psalm (cf. p. 13) has the theme of fertility, which would fit a setting in the autumnal festival. It is often used at

144

Christian weddings. Man and wife, work and home, are all blessed by God if his will for them is obeyed.

Second Reading   **Hebrews 2: 9–11**

The unity of mankind is in fact ruined by sin, and man is victim to suffering and death. So God sends Jesus to draw the human race together again. He does not make a fresh start, but begins where we are, becoming a brother man and undergoing suffering and death for man's sin. But this leads him to eternal life, from which he can become the first perfect man, able to transmit his own qualities to men everywhere. All who will do so can become united to him, receive his virtues and follow his lead. He becomes the head of a renewed humanity, and God wonderfully brings about his original purpose.

Gospel   **Mark 10: 2–16**

Here are two incidents in Jesus' ministry where he affirms both marriage and children, thus reaffirming the Genesis story.

The Mosaic Law permitted a man to divorce his wife, but there was great diversity of opinion in Jesus' time about the legitimate reasons for doing so. Here the Pharisees try to test his orthodoxy, and he typically throws the question back at them – they know perfectly well what the Mosaic Law says. But, again typically, he goes behind the Law to the fundamental principle stated in Genesis. Whatever concession the Law may have allowed their frailties, God's will is clearly that divorce should never be necessary. Then to his disciples he puts it in even stronger terms.

The second incident shows Jesus' love for children, and his faith in their basic trustfulness (so often, alas, betrayed), which is the attitude all men need if they are to enter God's kingdom.

Twenty-eighth Sunday in Ordinary Time

To have Christ is to have the greatest possible riches.

First Reading   **Wisdom 7: 7–11**

In the latter Old Testament period some Jewish writers practically personified God's Wisdom. (The Christian idea of Jesus as God's eternal Word, as in John 1, was in part based upon this.) Wisdom was not merely intellectual; it was true understanding about life and how it should be lived. This poem sings the praises of Wisdom as the only true riches, all earthly treasure being worthless in comparison. (There is no implication that the earthly things are intrinsically bad; they simply pale into nothing in the light of Wisdom.) Christians of course apply the passage to Christ.

Responsorial Psalm   **90 (89)**

℟ *Fill us with your love that we may rejoice.*

1 Make us know the shortness of our life
   that we may gain wisdom of heart.
   Lord, relent! Is your anger for ever?
   Show pity to your servants. (R)

2 In the morning, fill us with your love;
   we shall exult and rejoice all our days.
   Give us joy to balance our affliction
   for the years when we knew misfortune. (R)

3 Show forth your work to your servants;
   let your glory shine on their children.
   Let the favour of the Lord be upon us;
   give success to the work of our hands. (R)

In this communal lament (cf. p. 12) the people pray for the ending of some long affliction. But more, it is a prayer for 'wisdom of heart', the only means of true happiness and success.

Second Reading   **Hebrews 4: 12–13**

The 'word of God' in the thought of this 'letter' to Hebrews may be described as God's Wisdom in its outgoing activity. It has its terrible as well as its bountiful side, for it sees into the smallest recesses, physical and spiritual, of the whole creation. God gives his riches to all who will take them, but he also makes his equally boundless demands upon all. The ultimate wealth is to know God, but this means being known by him – being open to him and ready to let him see and deal with all that is in us, both good and bad. The generosity of God is not an easy-going indulgence.

Gospel   Mark: 10: 17–30

A three-part story about wealth. First, the rich young man, who has led a virtuous life, comes and asks what he needs to do to get eternal life. Jesus sees what he is, and loves him; then makes the great demand that he should forsake all his possessions and follow Jesus. We may surmise that Jesus saw him as far advanced in goodness, and so ready for the next great step; perhaps he also saw that for this man this was the only way forward. Indeed, we may reflect, when Jesus was on earth, what else could anyone do who really wanted eternal life, but leave all and be with him? However, the man is too attached to the lower riches, and does not see their comparative worthlessness.

Jesus now applies the point generally. The rich find it uniquely hard to give themselves wholly to God. But – as the disciples see – the rich are only an extreme case, since God demands the same unreserved allegiance from all men. Only God's power, says Jesus, can suffice to bring a man to him.

But we, says Peter, have done just what you told the young man to do. Jesus answers with the paradox about self-giving to God. Give yourself to him without holding anything back, and you will receive his boundless gifts. God asks all, but gives all.

Twenty-ninth Sunday in Ordinary Time

The theme today is the redemptive suffering of Christ.

First Reading   Isaiah 53: 10–11

This is part of the fourth Suffering Servant song (see 24th Sunday). The suffering has had a purpose: it has atoned for the sins of men, and justified many, because the Servant has identified himself with the sin that separated them from God. 'Atone' means to bring into one – God and man have been reunited. 'Justify' means to acquit someone, to declare him to be in the right; man has been acquitted of his sin and is in the right with God.

The Servant does not only suffer, however. After his suffering is complete, he has the joy of seeing its effects upon his 'heirs' – those to whom he has bequeathed salvation.

Responsorial Psalm   33 (32)

℟ *May your love be upon us, O Lord,*
  as we place all our hope in you.

1 The word of the Lord is faithful
  and all his works to be trusted.
  The Lord loves justice and right
  and fills the earth with his love. (R)

2 The Lord looks on those who revere him,
  on those who hope in his love,
  to rescue their souls from death,
  to keep them alive in famine. (R)

3 Our soul is waiting for the Lord.
  The Lord is our help and our shield.
  May your love be upon us, O Lord,
  as we place all our hope in you. (R)

A good example of an Israelite hymn (cf. p. 12), this Psalm tells of God's loving help for men, which was at work in his Servant (whom we see as Jesus).

148

Second Reading   **Hebrews 4: 14–16**

Once a year in the Temple (and in the Tent before the Temple was built), on the Day of Atonement, the High Priest offered sacrifice for Israel's sins, and then entered the inmost shrine of God's presence. Hebrews represents Jesus as doing in reality what the High Priest did by analogy. In his own death he offered the perfect sacrifice, of himself, for the sins of all mankind, and then entered the presence of God in heaven itself, to be a mediator between God and us.

He could do this because he identified himself with the weaknesses and temptations of men, and knows what it is to be a man. Now, like the Servant, he rejoices to see all that his suffering has achieved.

Gospel   **Mark 10: 35–45**

James and John have no real idea of what following Jesus will mean for them. They ask for the most honourable positions in his Kingdom – but the way into that Kingdom for Jesus will be suffering and death (he alludes to this as the 'cup' he later prays to be saved from in Gethsemane, and as the 'baptism he must be baptized with' in Luke 12: 50). Whether or not they understand the allusions, they boldly claim that they can go through what Jesus has to go through; and Jesus promises that they shall – all his disciples must follow his path of death. But all of them will equally follow him into his glory, and James and John will be like the rest, not above them.

The brothers' request has angered the other disciples, so Jesus spells out the right attitude for them all. For his followers the only supremacy is the supremacy of loving service; his own supremacy is that he has given himself entirely for the loving service of mankind.

Thirtieth Sunday in Ordinary Time

The theme is God's wonderful restoration of fallen mankind.

First Reading   Jeremiah 31: 7–9

Jeremiah prophesied after the northern kingdom of Israel (as distinct from the southern kingdom of Judah) had been conquered by the Assyrians in 721 BC, its capital city Samaria destroyed, and its inhabitants deported to Assyria.

His message is that God will rescue the exiles and bring them back to a restored and united Israel. This did not in fact occur historically, but Christians hold that it did occur in a more important way, when Christ came to restore all mankind to unity with one another in himself – in what is rightly called the 'new Israel', his Church. We therefore take Jeremiah's words as prophesying the ultimate unity of mankind in the body of Christ.

Responsorial Psalm   126 (125)

℟ *What marvels the Lord worked for us!*
Indeed we were glad.

1 When the Lord delivered Zion from bondage,
   It seemed like a dream.
   Then was our mouth filled with laughter,
   on our lips there were songs. (R)

2 The heathens themselves said: 'What marvels
   the Lord worked for them!'
   What marvels the Lord worked for us!
   Indeed we were glad. (R)

3 Deliver us, O Lord, from our bondage
   as streams in dry land.
   Those who are sowing in tears
   will sing when they reap. (R)

4 They go out, they go out, full of tears,
   carrying seed for the sowing:
   they come back, they come back, full of song,
   carrying their sheaves. (R)

This Psalm originally referred to the historical restoration of

Jerusalem, which like Samaria had been destroyed; it was subsequently rebuilt under Nehemiah. So God has turned sorrow into joy.

Second Reading   **Hebrews 5: 1–6**

Once again Hebrews shows how God ultimately answered the hopes and predictions of the prophets and Psalms. He provided the perfect man who lived and died in full accord with his will; who then entered heaven as the one true man, yet eternally united to God; and who now represents man to God, as the Jewish High Priest represented Israel. Aaron was the first High Priest according to Leviticus; but Melchizedek was God's priest long before that, as we read in Genesis 14. Moreover, Psalm 110, quoted here, sees Melchizedek as the archetypal high priest, and predicts that the Messiah will be such a priest also; for Christians, then, the Psalm is fulfilled in Jesus. He represents us in heaven, and as we are joined to him God brings us all into restored unity and joy.

Gospel   **Mark 10: 46–52**

God's restoring work was already going on in Jesus' earthly ministry. When Jesus forgave or healed he was doing for particular people what God wills to do for all, and each healing is a sign of hope for the ultimate healing of man's division from God and within himself.

The story, however, reads not like a mere example, but like the earthly and lively 'piece of real life' it is. It helps us to see that God works in the here and now, with real people, with their peculiar and sometimes entertaining characteristics. God performed his saving work in the world we live in, for people like us.

Thirty-first Sunday in Ordinary Time

God's supreme demand is love.

First Reading   **Deuteronomy 6: 2–6**

'Moses' is represented as giving Israel his last teachings before they
enter the Promised Land, and here he tells them the fundamental
relationship to God which must govern their whole lives. They must
'fear' him (meaning not terror, but the fear and awe that the creature
must owe the Creator and Judge of all). They must obey him (by
'keeping and observing' what he has commanded them through
Moses). But above all they must love him with every part of their
being.

Here is one of the places where the New Testament teaches
nothing beyond the Old: Jesus quotes it as the greatest commandment. What is new is that Jesus carries it out, with all its demands.

Responsorial Psalm   **18 (17)**

℞ *I love you, Lord, my strength.*

1 I love you, Lord, my strength,
    my rock, my fortress, my saviour.
    My God is the rock where I take refuge;
    my shield, my mighty help, my stronghold.
    The Lord is worthy of all praise:
    when I call I am saved from my foes. (R)

2 Long life to the Lord, my rock!
    Praised be the God who saves me.
    He has given great victories to his king
    and shown his love for his anointed. (R)

A Psalm of thanksgiving in which the king praises God for an
experience of salvation and testifies to its various aspects before the
assembled worshippers. Our love for God is not the love of equals,
but of weak men for the strong and gracious God.

Second Reading   **Hebrews 7: 23–28**

Here are further aspects of Christ's heavenly priesthood. Since he is beyond death, he can never cease to represent and intercede for us; men can always find their way to God through him.

His perfection ensures his unity with God, and this gives imperfect men their assurance that they really get to God through him. In this one respect he differs from them, but that does not break his unity with them. Thus he genuinely unites sinful men and perfect God, being himself human yet perfect.

We can apply this to the question of loving God. Jesus alone of men loved God perfectly, but in him we learn to love God better. His perfection gives us confidence, frees us from anxiety, and lets us get on with the business of growing in love for God.

Gospel   **Mark 12: 28–34**

We read a number of stories of Jesus being questioned – sometimes maliciously, sometimes with goodwill – and returning a brilliant answer that leaves his hearers speechless. In this case the scribe (a trained and qualified expert on the Law of Moses) turns out to be a man of goodwill whom Jesus praises warmly.

The first commandment is part of what we read in Deuteronomy. Then Jesus goes further than the original question, and gives the second commandment: love your fellow man. This is also from the Law, in Leviticus 19: 18. Jesus quotes the Law, but with his own authority establishes what is supreme in it. The scribe agrees, and adds that this surpasses all the externals of religion. No one else dares say another word.

Thirty-second Sunday in Ordinary Time

The generosity of self-giving love.

First Reading   **1 Kings 17: 10–16**

There is a great drought. Elijah asks the widow for a little water, and she goes to fetch some; he asks even more and she explains that she is about to cook, for her son and herself, the last food they have. Her generosity will in fact accelerate her own death; she is literally loving another even at the cost of dying sooner than she might – loving her neighbour as herself.

Her great love is rewarded by a miracle which ensures that she does not die, but survives till the drought is over. Generosity is answered by generosity. We cannot but see her as a type of Christ who gave all and received all, in dying and being raised from death.

Responsorial Psalm   **146 (145)**

℟ *My soul, give praise to the Lord.*
  or *Alleluia!*

1 It is the Lord who keeps faith for ever,
  who is just to those who are oppressed.
  It is he who gives bread to the hungry,
  the Lord, who sets prisoners free. (R)

2 It is the Lord who gives sight to the blind,
  who raises up those who are bowed down.
  It is the Lord who loves the just,
  the Lord, who protects the stranger. (R)

3 He upholds the widow and orphan
  but thwarts the path of the wicked.
  The Lord will reign for ever,
  Zion's God, from age to age. (R)

This hymn has more than an element of instruction. God cares for all who suffer. We may not see his ways, and we may have to wait for his final reign; but we can trust him to save us.

Second Reading   **Hebrews 9: 24–28**

The chief point for us here is the inward disposition of Christ which enabled his death to be the means of our salvation. It is his 'sacrificing himself'; he 'offers himself'; it is his generous self-giving love. In his case it was shown supremely in his death, which 'does away sin' and 'takes the faults of many on himself'. Many ways of explaining how such sin-bearing actually works have been offered us, but none removes a deep element of mystery, and often metaphor and imagery seem more adequate than theology. But what is quite clear is that it was possible because Jesus loved; there is nothing obscure about that. He gave all for love of God and man. And then he received all from God's love, and rejoices when he receives our love.

Gospel   **Mark 12: 38–44**

The second part of the Gospel corresponds to the first reading. Here is another widow who gives all she has, this time in the form of her last money, put into the alms-box in the Temple. The rich gave more, but only what was left over from their other spending; her little is her all. Jesus says it was all she had to live on, so she too has in effect offered her life to God.

The first part makes a contrast between her and the hypocrisy of the scribes who make the most of the honour paid to them as experts in the Law of Moses, but impoverish widows (probably by receiving gifts from them). They remind us of Elijah's apparent readiness to impoverish the widow he met; but that was to very different effect.

(We must note that it is not implied that all scribes were like the ones here denounced by Jesus.)

Thirty-third Sunday in Ordinary Time

In the end God's purpose will be achieved.

First Reading   **Daniel 12: 1–3**

Both Old and New Testaments tell of the End, when God will finally conquer evil and receive the perfect love and worship he deserves. They cannot express such eternal finalities except in visions and images that stretch what we know to a size beyond the normal. Daniel is the chief Old Testament book of this type of literature, technically termed 'apocalyptic'. The form and details of apocalyptic are secondary, but the message is ultimate: God will triumph in the end.

Apocalyptic books were written in times of persecution and oppression, to keep hope alive. Here Daniel affirms that though terrible distress is to come, Israel, under the protection of the angel Michael, will be delivered by God, and right will triumph.

Responsorial Psalm   **16 (15)**

℟ *Preserve me, God, I take refuge in you.*

1 O Lord, it is you who are my portion and cup;
 it is you yourself who are my prize.
 I keep the Lord ever in my sight:
 since he is at my right hand, I shall stand firm. (R)

2 And so my heart rejoices, my soul is glad;
 even my body shall rest in safety.
 For you will not leave my soul among the dead,
 nor let your beloved know decay. (R)

3 You will show me the path of life,
 the fullness of joy in your presence,
 at your right hand happiness for ever. (R)

This Psalm may have been used originally as the prayer of a king in connection with some atonement ceremonies. The psalmist trusts that God will finally bring him to eternal joy in his presence.

Second Reading **Hebrews 10: 11–14, 18**

Christ, eternally with the Father, has attained the final destiny of man. There is now the long interim period ('AD') when mankind, or that part of mankind which desires to, catches up with him. His followers are being sanctified – gradually becoming like him. His enemies – all who oppose him – will finally be subjected, like a stool under his feet. So, although the essential event has happened already, its final effects still lie far in the future.

Gospel **Mark 13: 24–32**

Jesus uses apocalyptic methods to teach about the End, and there is the same difficulty in distinguishing the essential message from its imagery. He teaches that God will complete his work through the Son of Man – a title often on his lips and probably an oblique way of referring to himself (see next Sunday's first reading). Some suggest that he did not consciously identify himself with the Son of Man, but that the early Church saw the identity. The chief point for us is plain enough: Christ who began God's work on earth, and continues it in heaven, will complete it.

He says that it will occur within his own generation, which on the face of it did not happen. He may, like the apocalyptists generally, have expressed the *certainty* of judgement (the essential point) by saying that it would come *soon*. Or, more subtly, he may have been expressing, in apocalyptic form, the significance of his coming death, which would be the deepest judgement upon the sins of the world, and the means of 'gathering his chosen' together.

Christ the King (Last Sunday of the year)

This solemnity of Christ the Universal King widens our horizons, to see life and power and authority in the perspective of eternity.

First Reading   Daniel 7: 13–14

'One like a son of man' meant one like a man, and not, as with the four previous apparitions in Daniel's vision, like various beasts. The one like a man represents Israel (as v. 27 subsequently shows), finally free from oppressive conquerers, and given authority to rule on God's behalf. Later Jewish writers used the phrase to mean a supernatural individual wielding God's power, and Jesus may have done the same, probably referring to himself. He was, we believe, the only true Israelite, just as he was the only true man. In Christian tradition, therefore, this passage is a foretelling of Jesus' exaltation to share God's sovereignty, as mankind and Israel had been intended to do.

Responsorial Psalm   93 (92)

℞ *The Lord is king, with majesty enrobed.*

1 The Lord is king, with majesty enrobed;
   the Lord has robed himself with might,
   he has girded himself with power. (R)

2 The world you made firm, not to be moved;
   your throne has stood firm from of old,
   From all eternity, O Lord, you are. (R)

3 Truly your decrees are to be trusted.
   Holiness is fitting to your house,
   O Lord, until the end of time. (R)

This Psalm gives a concentrated and dramatic presentation of God as Creator-king. The Lord reigns in nature – and, through his Law, in the hearts of men.

Second Reading   Revelation (Apocalypse) 1: 5–8

The Apocalypse is the New Testament equivalent of the book of Daniel, to which it often alludes; so here we have a Christian version of the first reading's vision. It is Jesus who is universal King and Judge, but it was through death and resurrection that he became so. He shares his royal and priestly work with his people, who act for him in the world, conquering the hearts of men, interceding for them in all their needs. In the end, we may say, Daniel's 'son of man' is indeed Israel, but the new Israel which is Christ and all who are his.

The last sentence, however, reminds us that all rests ultimately upon the timeless and boundless sovereignty of God himself. Alpha and omega are the first and last letters of the Greek alphabet: God is King from first to last, eternally and universally.

Gospel   **John 18: 33–37**

The language of sovereignty is so tainted by the abuse of power among human rulers that it needs purification. Jesus answers Pilate guardedly for this very reason. He has been accused of claiming political kingship of the Jews, but that is not his kind of kingdom. He will not contradict Pilate's statement that he is a king, but he must explain what sort. He wields power, but not by force: it is by uttering the truth of God, which rules men's hearts by its inherent attraction.

Christ's kingship thus has nothing of the despot or the dictator about it. He rules by truth and love, and so must those who rule in his name. Neither on earth nor in eternity will God force our allegiance, even though he is sovereign of all.

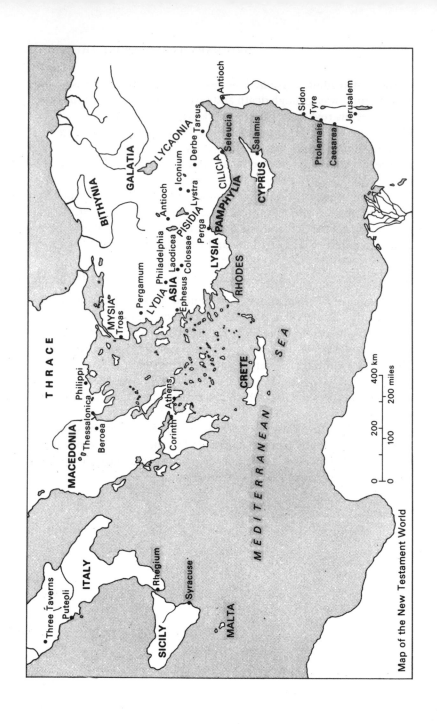

Map of the New Testament World

Chronological Table I

A Chart of Old Testament History and Literature

The purpose of the chart is to help the reader by co-ordinating the history and the literature. It is not possible to be precise about the dates of the literature, nor does a suggested date rule out the possibility of additions to completed books (as evidenced by the additions to Daniel and Esther in the Greek versions).

History	Literature
1 The Patriarchal Age (2000*–1300* BC)	
2 The Age of Moses, Joshua and Judges (1300*–1000* BC)	Judges ch. 5 1100*
3 Samuel, Saul, David and Solomon (1050–931)	Oldest of the Psalms and other poetry 1200–950*
4 Pre-exilic Period (931–587)	Oldest prose parts of the Pentateuch (950–850)
a. The Divided Monarchy	Amos 760–750*
b. The Assyrian destruction of the Northern Kingdom 722/721	Hosea 745–725*
	Isaiah 740–701*
	Early prose parts of Joshua–Judges–Samuel–Kings 800–700*
	Micah 725–690*
c. Reign of Josiah 640–609	Zephaniah 630–625*
	Habakkuk 625–600*
	First edition of Deuteronomy and deuteronomic writings
d. The Fall of Assyrian Nineveh to the Babylonians 612 BC	Nahum 612–610*
	Jeremiah 626–586
e. The Babylonian Invasion of Judah 598	
f. Destruction of Judah and the exile to Babylonia 587	

* *approximate dates*

5 The Exilic Period (587–539)

a. The Persian conquest of
   Babylonia 539
b. The Return from Exile 539*–516

6 The Post-Exilic Period (530*–
   167)
a. Persian Period 538–333
b. Careers of Ezra and Nehemiah
   450*

c. Greek Period 333–167

Passages in Jeremiah
Ezekiel 593*–560*
Second Isaiah (40–55) 550*–520*

Further compilations of elements in
Pentateuch
Haggai 520
Zechariah 520–518
Malachi, Joel(?), Obadiah 500–450*
Third Isaiah (?) 500–450
Priestly completion of the Penta-
teuch 450–400*
Compilation of Proverbs 400*
Job 450–350* (or possibly earlier)
Jonah, Ruth 425*
Ezra–Nehemiah–Chronicles 375–250*
Possible final editing of prophetic
books
Ecclesiastes 275–250*
Translation of the Pentateuch into
Greek 250*
Daniel 165*

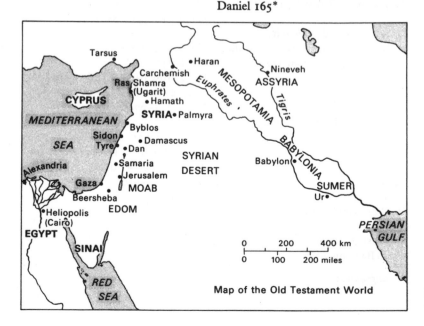

Map of the Old Testament World

Chronological Table II

A Chart of New Testament History and Literature

It is generally accepted that all the New Testament works were written before c. 125, though it is difficult to be specific and dates given, therefore, are approximate.

Church History and Literature		Jewish History	
Birth of Jesus	6–4 BC (?)	Herod the Gt	37–4 BC
		Herod Antipas (Tetrarch of Galilee)	4 BC–AD 39
		Archelaus (Ethnarch in Judea)	4 BC–AD 6
		Philip (Ethnarch of Ituraea)	4 BC–AD 34
		Caiaphas (High Priest)	AD 18–36
		Pontius Pilate (Roman Procurator in Judea)	26–36
Preaching of John the Baptist	27 (?)		
Ministry of Jesus	28–29 (?)		
Conversion of Paul	33–35 (?)		
		Herod Agrippa (King of Judea; from 41 king of the whole country)	37–44
James, son of Zebedee, executed; Peter imprisoned	41 (?)		
Paul in S. Galatia	47–49 (?)		
Paul in Corinth	50–51		
1 Thessalonians	51		
2 Thessalonians	51		
Paul in Ephesus	52–54	M. Antonius Felix (Procurator in Judea)	52–60
		M. Julius Agrippa II (Part of Galilee and	
Galatians	54–57	Peraea)	53
Paul arrested in Jerusalem	56		

1 Corinthians	57		
2 Corinthians	57		
Romans	58		
Philippians late 50's early 60's			
		Porcius Festus (Procurator in Judea)	60–61
Paul in Rome	60		
Philemon	61–63		
Ephesians*	61–63		
Colossians*	61–63		
James	62 (?)		
Death of James	62		
1 Peter	64 (?)		
Martyrdom of Peter and Paul	64 (?)		
MARK	65		
1 Timothy*	65		
Titus*	65		
2 Timothy*	66–67		
Christians flee to Pella	66–67		
Hebrews	60's (?)	Jewish war with Rome	66–70
		Fall of Jerusalem	70
MATTHEW	70's, 80's (?)		
LUKE	70's, 80's (?)	Masada falls; end of Jewish	
Acts	70's, 80's (?)	revolt	73
Jude	70's, 90's (?)		
James	80's (?)		
Hebrews	80's (?)		
JOHN	90's		
1 John	90's		
2 John	90's		
3 John	90's		
Apocalypse (Revelation)	90's		
2 Peter	100–125	Synod of Jamnia (fixed Old Testament Canon)	c. 100

*Authorship of these epistles questioned. If not Pauline then a later date, approx. 80's, is assigned.